SELF-GUIDED
TOUR OF
THE BIBLE

CHRISTOPHER D. HUDSON

Cristina esta guía de un recorrido por la biblia no lo he leido. Simplemente lo he revisado de forma general y rápida., sin embargo, la escogencia se debió a que el título me cautivó y pensé en ese Recorrido que ofrece, se puede aprender mucho que contribuya a nuestra edificación espiritual.

Espero te sea útil.

HENDRICKSON PUBLISHERS ROSE PUBLISHING

Peabody, Massachusetts

Self-Guided Tour of the Bible
© Copyright 2016 Christopher D. Hudson
Rose Publishing, LLC
P.O. Box 3473
Peabody, Massachusetts 01961-3473 USA
www.HendricksonRose.com

Hudson Bible writing team: Christopher D. Hudson, Peter DeHaan, and Len Woods

Published in association with The Steve Laube Agency, Phoenix, AZ

Cover design by Kent Jensen; layout design by Sergio Urquiza and Axel Shields

Maps: ©Michael Schmeling, www.aridocean.com

Library of Congress Cataloging-in-Publication Data

Names: Hudson, Christopher D., author.
Title: Self-guided tour of the Bible / Christopher D. Hudson.
Description: Carson, California : Rose Publishing, Inc., 2016.
Identifiers: LCCN 2016023191 (print) | LCCN 2016024776 (ebook) | ISBN
   9781628623550 | ISBN 9781628623567 ()
Subjects: LCSH: Bible--Introductions.
Classification: LCC BS475.3 .H83 2016 (print) | LCC BS475.3 (ebook) | DDC
   220.6/1--dc23
LC record available at https://lccn.loc.gov/2016023191

Printed in the United States of America
030917VP

Contents

Introduction: A Self-Guided Tour of God's Word 4

Chapter 1
Diving In: A Quick Overview of the Bible 9

Chapter 2
Getting Your Bearings: Basic Bible Geography 33

Chapter 3
Grasping the Story: A Time Line of Bible History 59

Chapter 4
Meeting the Characters: A Who's Who of Bible People 77

Chapter 5
Exploring the Content: A Breakdown of Bible Books 103

Chapter 6
Getting to the Heart of the Bible: Jesus' Life and Teachings 149

Chapter 7
Connecting the Dots: Jesus throughout the Bible......................... 173

Chapter 8
Peeking into the Future: Heaven, Hell, and Eternity 187

Chapter 9
Summarizing the Message: Major Themes in the Bible 203

Afterword... 225

Acknowledgments 226

For Further Reading... 227

Index 228

Introduction

A Self-Guided Tour of God's Word

The Bible can be an intimidating book.

For one thing, it's just plain *massive*. Consider that the best-selling novel *To Kill a Mockingbird* contains around 99,000 words. Dickens's heftier *A Tale of Two Cities* has 135,000 words. Now consider that the Bible has around *800,000* words!

The epic *War and Peace* by Tolstoy? It's more than 1,000 pages in length—and *still* around 200,000 words shorter than the Bible!

(Did we mention the Bible is big?)

Also the Bible can be *mysterious*. Where to start? What's an Old Testament and how does it differ from the New? What are we to make of all those exotic settings, strange events, and quirky characters?

We created this book to help with questions like that.

Imagine entering a vast museum dedicated to helping people understand the Bible. You might get lost wandering around all those vast exhibit halls—*unless* you had a handy-dandy guide.

Think of this book as such a resource. Think of each chapter as a clear, concise guide to some particular aspect of the Bible.

The beauty of a guide like this? You get to tour the "museum" at your own pace. You can follow the suggested order (1 through 9), but you surely don't have to. You get to decide which Bible "exhibit" you want to look at first and where you want to go next.

It's all up to you. What about the Bible has got you most curious?

As a kind of museum guide to the Bible, the chapters of this book function as overviews of nine important, different rooms.

Now, if you've ever been to a world-class museum, you know you can't see (much less appreciate) everything in a single day. In the same way, you can't learn everything about the Bible in a short time.

But that's okay. It's by returning again and again over the course of a lifetime that we not only increase our understanding of God's Word but also come to know the Author himself! There are always new things to discover.

Here are some tips for your tour:

- **Decide how much interest and time you have.** If you are new or fairly new to the Bible—or if you are pushed for time—you may simply want a better understanding of the essential story of the Bible. You can do that by going to rooms 1, 3, and 6. Or, if you have doubts about the trustworthiness of the Bible, you may want to visit rooms 1 and 7 first.

■ **Go at your own pace.** There's no right (or wrong) way to read this book. And there's no prize for finishing quickly. Take your time.

■ **Keep your Bible handy (and open).** This book is designed to be read *alongside the Bible*. Look up in your Bible all the references you find here. As you do, your understanding will grow.

■ **Mark up this book.** Write down your observations and questions. The Bible is like a priceless painting. Every time you look into it, you'll see and experience new insights. Jot these down, so you can come back to them.

■ **Check the resource list** at the end of this book for any areas you want to explore in more detail. While this book covers a lot of ground, it is only an introduction. Want to go deeper? We'll point out some helps for further study.

■ **Share what you learn with others.** Learning is best retained when we share what we've learned with others. Find a classmate, family member, or friend to read with and compare notes. Or share with a spouse or child the most interesting things you learn along the way. You'll pass on knowledge to them and retain more for yourself in the process.

Before you begin your tour, it's important to understand our approach in writing this book. We believe the Bible is a reliable word, or message, from the Almighty himself. God wanted to reveal truths about himself, about us, and about the meaning of life. And so he did—speaking to and through people. The result is the Bible.

We also believe the best, most accurate understanding of a Bible passage is usually the most straightforward one. And so we constantly ask, "God, what are you saying through this verse or that passage?" Rather than using the Bible to justify ideas (or biases) we already have, we try to humbly and prayerfully listen to God's voice. This book simply provides background material and practical tips to help you learn how to do that yourself.

As you take this self-guided tour, it's our prayer that you'll develop a deeper appreciation and better understanding of the treasure chest that is the Bible. More than that, we pray you'll get to know God in a richer way.

Thanks for taking this tour. May God bless you as you read, engage, and apply his Word.

Christopher D. Hudson and the Hudson Bible Team
www.ReadEngageApply.com
Facebook.com/Christopher.D.Hudson.books
Twitter: @ReadEngageApply

Chapter 1

DIVING IN: A QUICK OVERVIEW OF THE BIBLE

Exhibit Hall 5
Exploring the
Content:
A Breakdown
of Bible Books

Exhibit Hall 7
Connecting
the Dots:
Jesus throughout
the Bible

Exhibit Hall 4
Meeting the
Characters:
A Who's Who
of Bible People

Exhibit Hall 8
Peeking into
the Future:
Heaven, Hell, and
Eternity

Exhibit Hall 6
Getting to the Heart
of the Bible:
Jesus' Life and Teachings

Exhibit Hall 3
Grasping the Story:
A Time Line
of Bible History

Exhibit Hall 9
Summarizing
the Message:
Major Themes
in the Bible

Exhibit Hall 2
Getting Your
Bearings:
Basic Bible Geography

Exhibit Hall 1
Diving In:
A Quick Overview
of the Bible

You are here.

The Bible.

The best-selling book in the history of the world is venerated and vilified, beloved and burned. Some—who regard it as God's Word—swear *by* it. Others—who regard it as a dangerous man-made document—swear *at* it.

As we start our tour, let's begin with the audacious claim that the book we call the Bible is not just any book. *The Christian view is that the Bible is actually God's Word.*

- Is that claim true?
- Is the Bible itself true?
- Can we really trust it?
- Can it really transform us?

This chapter of your Bible tour guidebook is designed to help you wrestle with five basic but very important questions:

1. What role did God play in the writing of the Bible?

2. Who were the human authors of the Bible?

3. How did the Bible get to us?

4. How do we know what the Bible means?

5. Why are the different parts of the Bible so, well, different?

1. What role did God play in the writing of the Bible?

We mentioned a couple of classic literary works—*To Kill a Mockingbird* and *A Tale of Two Cities*. Many would say those works are *inspiring*. But the claim of the Bible is that it is *inspired*.

"All Scripture is inspired by God and profitable for teaching, for reproof, for correction, for training in righteousness." —2 Timothy 3:16 NASB

Exhibit Hall 1

The idea in 2 Timothy 3:16 is that the Bible is "God-breathed," that is, inspired. That's a way of saying the Bible finds its origin in God himself. This obviously doesn't mean God sat down at a physical desk and used ink to write words on parchment. To say that the Bible is *inspired* means that in a mysterious and hard-to-comprehend way, God superintended human authors. He worked with and through their unique personalities, styles, and vocabularies so that they recorded the things he wanted them to convey to the world.

Inspiration is a bold claim. It's a jaw-dropping thing to suggest that a perfect God would partner with imperfect humans to reveal his nature and will. But Christians believe he did. That's what we mean when we say the Bible is inspired. It's not just any book.

Sometimes the human writers of Scripture wrote down their experiences from God-given visions—Ezekiel 37, for example, or most of the book of Revelation. In other places, we see the phrase "this is what the LORD says" (for example, Isaiah 18:4; Jeremiah 6:16) followed by verbatim statements from God. These instances are similar to a scribe taking dictation.

However, the great differences in writing style throughout the Bible show us that God didn't primarily dictate to copyists. He spoke to and through human authors.

Peter was a follower of Christ and a leader in the early church. He was also one of these collaborators with God in the writing of Scripture. (He wrote the New Testament letters 1 and 2 Peter.)

Synonyms for the Bible

You'll hear people refer to the Bible in a number of ways:

- Scripture
- God's Word
- The Holy Bible
- God's Revelation
- Holy Writ
- The Word of God
- The Word
- The Good Book
- The Old and New Testaments
- Biblical Truth

Exhibit Hall 1

Peter described that process like this:

> "For prophecy never had its origin in the human will, but prophets, though human, spoke from God as they were carried along by the Holy Spirit."
> —2 Peter 1:21

Bible Fact

The Old Testament (the first thirty-nine books of the Bible) was originally written (roughly 1500–400 BC) mainly in Hebrew, with some Aramaic. The New Testament (the final twenty-seven books of the Bible) was written (approximately AD 50–100) in Greek. This means the various writers of the Bible not only had their own communication styles but also used different languages.

The verb for "carried along" was used in ancient times to describe a ship being driven by a strong wind (see Acts 27:15, 17). The sailors in such conditions, no matter how skilled, could not ultimately determine the ship's course. The sailors were active and involved. They played a real role. But in the end, it was the wind that controlled the destination of the ship.

This is a good picture of the writing of the Bible. Both God and people were involved in its production, but God was the ultimate author. He directed the writing. The content is the divine author's; the stylistic differences are due to the human authors. Two things are true:

1. People played a vital role in the production of the Bible.

2. The final product is ultimately from God. This is why we call the Bible God's Word.

Old and New Testaments: What's the Difference?

Exhibit Hall 1

Old Testament	New Testament
39 books	27 books
Written from approximately 1450 to 420 BC	Written from approximately AD 44 to 96
Humanity's need for redemption	God's provision of redemption
Preparing the way for Christ	Presenting the way of Christ
A Savior is promised, hinted at, alluded to	A Savior is given, hated, killed, resurrected, ascended, and proclaimed
The law is emphasized	Grace is emphasized
Animal sacrifices made repeatedly to temporarily forgive sin	Christ sacrificed once-for-all to forever forgive sin
The twelve tribes of Israel are prominent	The twelve disciples of Christ are prominent
God wants to reveal his glory through Israel	God wants to reveal his glory through the church
Begins in a garden (Eden) with God's creation being ruined by sin	Ends with God's creation of a new heaven and a new earth completely devoid of sin because of Christ's sacrifice

In accepting that God inspired the words in the Bible, we acknowledge that it contains the very words of God. In saying this, we need to remember something else: God's unchanging nature. Both Moses and David speak of this (Numbers 23:19; Psalm 55:19). The implications are huge: The words of God from a few millennia ago are still words we can and should rely on today.

Since God doesn't change, his words and their meanings don't change. What he says in the Bible is still a trustworthy source for understanding reality, forming beliefs, and making decisions. The apostle Paul confirms the Bible's present-day relevancy when he reminds us that all Scripture (the Bible) is useful for teaching us, correcting us, and training us in how to live (2 Timothy 3:16).

And the bonus? Since the Bible is God's Word, engaging the Bible is an opportunity to engage with God. Although our knowledge of the Bible and of God will always be incomplete—until we one day meet him—the more we study the Bible, the more of God we can know now.

2. Who were the human authors of the Bible?

The Bible has about thirty to forty human authors. These writers came from varied backgrounds. There were shepherds (Moses and David), fishermen (Peter and John), a military leader (David), prophets (Isaiah and Jeremiah), kings (David and Solomon), a prime minister (Daniel), a royal cupbearer (Nehemiah), a doctor (Luke), a tax collector (Matthew), and a tent maker (Paul). Last, but most important, consider Jesus, a carpenter-turned-teacher. Though Jesus didn't write any of the books in the Bible, the books of Matthew, Mark, Luke, John, Acts, and Revelation all record his spoken words.

Author	Date Written*	Books
MOSES	1446–1406 BC	Genesis, Exodus, Leviticus, Numbers, and Deuteronomy
EZRA	457–444 BC	Possibly Ezra and possibly 1 and 2 Chronicles
NEHEMIAH	424–400 BC	Possibly Nehemiah
DAVID	1011–971 BC	73 psalms in the book of Psalms
SOLOMON	971–931 BC	Proverbs (with help on the last two chapters), Ecclesiastes, and Song of Songs
ISAIAH	701–681 BC	Isaiah
JEREMIAH	626–582 BC	Jeremiah and Lamentations
EZEKIEL	593–570 BC	Ezekiel
DANIEL	605–535 BC	Daniel
HOSEA	752–722 BC	Hosea
JOEL	Unknown, possibly 515–350 BC	Joel
AMOS	760–753 BC	Amos
OBADIAH	586 BC	Obadiah
JONAH	783–753 BC	Jonah
MICAH	738–698 BC	Micah
NAHUM	663–612 BC	Nahum
HABAKKUK	609–598 BC	Habakkuk
ZEPHANIAH	641–628 BC	Zephaniah
HAGGAI	520 BC	Haggai
ZECHARIAH	520–518 BC	Zechariah
MALACHI	400s BC	Malachi

Author	Date Written*	Books
MATTHEW	AD 50s–60s	Matthew
MARK	AD 50s–60s	Mark
LUKE	AD 60–62	Luke and Acts
JOHN	AD 85–96	John; 1, 2, and 3 John; and Revelation
PAUL	AD 48–66	Romans; 1 and 2 Corinthians; Galatians; Ephesians; Philippians; Colossians; 1 and 2 Thessalonians; 1 and 2 Timothy; Titus; Philemon; and possibly Hebrews
JAMES (JESUS' HALF-BROTHER)	AD 49	James
PETER	AD 64–65	1 and 2 Peter
JUDE	AD 60s–80s	Jude
UNKNOWN	Various	Joshua; Judges; Ruth; 1 and 2 Samuel; 1 and 2 Kings; Esther; Job; some psalms; and possibly Hebrews

*Dates are approximate.

2 TIMOTHY 3:16

16 All Scripture is God-breathed and is useful for teaching, rebuking, correcting and training in righteousness,

17 so that the servant of God may be thoroughly equipped for every good work

HOW TO FIND A VERSE IN THE BIBLE

You're reading along in this guide, and you come to a parenthetical note that looks like this: (2 Timothy 3:16).

That's simply a reference to a specific verse in the Bible. The "2" before "Timothy" means it's from the second letter to Timothy—sometimes it means it's a letter "by" someone. The "3" means it's found in the third chapter, and the "16" means you need to look for the sixteenth verse.

Use your Bible's table of contents until you become familiar with where the different books are found.

Note: The Bible's chapter and verse breakdowns weren't part of the original writings. Those were added in the fifteenth century as a help to students and readers of the Bible.

With so many writers, it's clear the Bible is an anthology: a collection of works from various contributors. Unlike many anthologies, though, the Bible has some unique traits. First, most of its contributors are not contemporaries with each other. Their contributions span centuries, likely some 1,500 years from start to finish.

It's also obvious these assorted individuals contributed different kinds of literature (a.k.a. *genres*). This is why the Bible contains:

- Stories (history/narratives)
- Poetry
- Prophecies of future events (apocalyptic literature)
- Portraits of Jesus (Gospels)
- A slew of messages to various churches and people (epistles)

Scattered among all these are messages, or sermons, given to God's people. Through each type of writing, we learn about God and our connection to him.

A close reading shows these writers have their own individual styles. Some are technical in their wording, while others use more common language. Some jump from topic to topic; others unfold logical arguments. Some writers repeat themselves; others are concise. We appreciate the Bible more when we understand each author's communication method and look past his stylistic preferences to understand God's message.

The Bible writers did their work in different settings. David composed many of his psalms while tending sheep or hiding from his enemies in the wilderness. Paul wrote some of his letters while on missionary journeys. When Paul was incarcerated, he sometimes dictated to a trusted colleague who sat outside his prison cell.

The writers of books like 1 and 2 Kings or 1 and 2 Chronicles were officials or priests who wanted to document the historical events of God's people. Others, like Luke (the Gospel writer), conducted thorough, historical research, interviewing multiple eyewitnesses. They then diligently recorded their findings in an effort to encourage future generations. Isaiah, Ezekiel, Daniel, and John all had incomprehensible visions and shared them the best they could.

Many of these individuals likely had no idea they were writing anything that would ever be considered sacred. All wrote because they felt compelled to do so. It's doubtful they envisioned the end result would one day be the big, thick book we call the Bible.

3. How did the Bible get to us?

So thirty to forty contributors independently writing over hundreds of years, all over the ancient Near East—how did their sixty-six writings get together in one book?

Over the centuries, these writings were collected and arranged and recognized as inspired, sacred authority by groups of scribes and scholars. The Old Testament priest Ezra is said to have collected and arranged various religious writings around 450 BC. In the first few centuries AD, the four Gospels as well as Paul's letters and other epistles were circulated among many church congregations and seen by Christians as authoritative. Near the end of the fourth century, in AD 397, a church council, the Synod of Carthage, confirmed the twenty-seven books of the New Testament based on precise spiritual criteria. It's crucial to understand that these scholars and church councils did not *make* a book become inspired. They didn't *bestow* that characteristic. On the contrary, they *recognized* that divine quality in certain writings.

Still, the question remains: All these things happened a long time ago—before the days of copy machines and printing presses—so how is it that we have the ancient writings of Moses and David?

Let's say you find some old newspapers in your attic. They're just fifty years old, but they're yellowed, faded, and torn. They look like something—bugs? a mouse?—has been chewing on them.

If that can happen in only a few decades to modern newsprint, how do we know what Moses wrote 3,400 years ago?

The short answer: copies!

Here's a little-known fact: *We don't have any of the original writings of the Bible.* It's true. We only have copies. Actually we have copies . . . of copies . . . of copies . . . of copies . . . (you get the idea).

Before the days of PDFs and copy machines, we had living, breathing copy machines! Copying was a full-time job for many people.

These copyists (often priests, later monks) were extremely careful in taking writings that had originally been committed to stone, clay, leather, papyrus, or animal skins and reproducing them for future generations. This was painstaking work. The copyists developed intricate methods of counting lines, words, and letters to guard against errors.

Did mistakes creep in? Of course. Humans make errors. Occasional misspellings would occur, and words would inadvertently get omitted. But with so many people making so many copies (more than 5,000 of which we still have), it becomes possible, through the science called *textual criticism*, to track back, find the probable source of the errors, compare manuscripts, and uncover what the original text likely said.

All this is to say: We can have confidence that our modern-day Bibles are a reliable expression of what God communicated to and through people like David and Moses.

WE CAN TRUST THE BIBLE

Those who copied the ancient Scriptures in the days before Xerox® were careful. How careful? Princeton's Bruce Metzger, one of the preeminent New Testament scholars of the twentieth century, concluded that after two thousand years of being copied exclusively by hand, only forty of the twenty thousand lines of the New Testament are in dispute. More importantly, none of these variances undermines the basic teachings of the Christian faith. In other words, our modern-day Bibles are *very* credible—far more so than any other ancient historical document.

Bible Fact

Maybe you've heard people speak of the canon of Scripture, or of the Bible books being canonical. The word *canon* comes from a Greek word that means "rule or measuring stick." Thus the sixty-six canonical books are the books that reveal God's rule of faith. Using those books, we can authoritatively and accurately know the truth about God.

For example, let's compare the works of the philosopher Plato to that of the New Testament writings.

Works of Plato	New Testament
Written around 400 BC.	Written between AD 49 and 96.
Only 210 copies have survived.	Well over 5,000 portions have survived. Fragments survive from a few decades after the texts were first written.
The earliest surviving manuscript was copied in AD 895, more than 1,200 years after the original documents were written.	Complete books survive from the second century, less than a century after the books were written.
	Complete manuscripts of the New Testament survive from the early fourth century, less than three centuries after the original documents were written.

(From *How We Got the Bible* by Timothy Paul Jones)

In 1946, something happened to give us even greater confidence in the accuracy of the Bible's reproduction. The Qumran texts, more commonly known as the Dead Sea Scrolls, were found by shepherds in a cave near the historic village of Khirbet Qumran, about a mile from the Dead Sea.

People from a monastic Jewish community who lived in the area (possibly the Essenes) likely hid the scrolls there to preserve them from being destroyed by the Roman army. This army indeed devastated the Jewish community in AD 68, but the scrolls survived.

It took a while before anyone realized the significance of the shepherds' find. Subsequent searches in the area over the next decade uncovered more caves and hundreds of well-preserved scrolls sealed in clay jars. Soon, parts of every Old Testament book (except Esther) had been found, with multiple copies of several books. Archaeologists hail this as one of the greatest discoveries of modern times.

Using carbon dating, these scrolls were found to be hundreds of years older than our oldest and best Old Testament copies at the time (i.e., from the ninth and tenth centuries AD).

The Great Isaiah Scroll of the Dead Sea Scrolls

Yet in comparing the older Dead Sea Scrolls with much more recent copies of the biblical text, there is remarkable, though not perfect, agreement. This confirms that highly accurate copies were made throughout history. This means we can have great confidence that what we read today in our Bibles is trustworthy.

4. How do we know what the Bible means?

Can a person jump into the Bible *anywhere* and begin to understand it?

Caves where some of the Dead Sea Scrolls were found

That's a tricky question. Could you start reading Tolstoy's *War and Peace* on page 511 and understand it? That might be tough. What if a friend blogs daily about ways to save money, and you only pay attention when she writes about *how to travel cheaply*. Could you understand those posts? Sure.

So the right answer is "It depends."

Here are some simple realities and reminders that can help as you jump into the Bible and seek to understand it. Follow the simple plan: read, engage, and apply.

READ

Reading is the first step to understanding. Here are several helpful tips and ideas:

- **Read a passage two or even three times.** Repetition is your often leads to "aha!" moments).

- **Take time to step back**, and read what's just before and just after your passage. Do this so that you'll understand the *context* of your passage, so you don't take things out of context.

- **Pay attention to words.** Underline the verbs to emphasize their importance. Look for key terms, repeated phrases, emphasized themes.

- **As you read, be like a detective** investigating a scene. Be curious. Gather facts by asking lots of questions: What does this passage actually say? What do I see? What's the setting? Who are the characters? What are they doing and saying?

- **Take plenty of notes.** Write down your observations.

FROM GOD TO US
How We Got the Bible

REVELATION
God unveils special, detailed truth about himself, humanity, and eternity to select individuals.

INSPIRATION
God oversees the recording of this truth so that his revelation is without errors in the original writings.

THE WORLD PROCLAMATION
Sharing God's truth with neighbors near and far!

DUPLICATION
Scribes and priests carefully hand copy these ancient documents on leather, papyrus, and vellum (animal skins).

ILLUMINATION & TRANSFORMATION
As people read the Bible in a language they can understand, the Holy Spirit opens their eyes to God's truth (that's illumination) and lives are forever changed (that's transformation)!

CANONIZATION
The process of church leaders collecting various religious writings and recognizing which ones bear the marks of inspiration (divine authenticity).

TRANSLATION
Scholars translate the Bible to make it understandable to more people. Missionaries spread God's Word.

PRESERVATION
Despite the efforts of some to destroy the Bible, God sovereignly ensures that his Word is guarded and passed on.

PUBLICATION
Thanks to Gutenberg's printing press, the Bible is published in 1455. No more hand copying!

Exhibit Hall 1

ENGAGE

Engaging is the second step of reading and understanding the Bible. This is where we move from simply seeing what the Bible *says* to grasping what the Bible *means*. These tips can help us better engage and interpret the text:

- **Pray for wisdom and insight.** Jesus promised that the Spirit would lead us into all truth (John 16:13). Who better than to help us understand God's Word than God's Spirit?

- **Let the Bible speak for itself.** Before you decide what you *think* a passage means, give the Bible the opportunity to explain itself. A cross-reference Bible can help. It lists in the margin (or sometimes in a center column) other verses in Scripture that address that same subject or use the same biblical word or phrase as the one in the verse you're reading. By looking up these companion or complementary passages, you'll get a richer, more accurate understanding of biblical topics.

- **Understand that Scripture will never contradict Scripture**, because God doesn't contradict himself. Certain passages may *seem* to contradict each other, but when we can't reconcile two passages, it's a "we" problem, not a "God" problem. Consult a Bible commentary only after you've read your passage several times and **prayed** for clarity.

Make Prayer a Priority

While reading the Bible on our own is a worthy pursuit, asking God to speak to us as we read can make our investment more valuable. God, through his Spirit, can show us deeper meaning when we read the text, just as he inspired the original authors when they wrote it. We need to make prayer a priority as we read and study the Bible. Our goal ought to be to discover God's meaning, not to bring our own meaning to the Bible.

Here are some suggestions:

* *Thank God for what he has revealed to you previously.*
* *Ask God to speak in the text you are about to read. Pray for focus. Ask God to provide new insights and build upon what you already know.*
* *Ask God for help as you encounter confusing passages. Pray for clarity and supernatural insight.*
* *Ask God to help you to apply his truth to your life.*
* *Prayer can help us ensure that we are focused on and determined to find God's words for us today.*

- **Don't read too much into unique or rare biblical events.** Much of the Bible consists of *descriptions* of events that took place, not necessarily *prescriptions* for how we should routinely live. For example, there's a story in Matthew about Jesus giving his follower Peter instructions for paying a temple tax: "Go to the lake and throw out your line. Take the first fish you catch; open its mouth and you will find a four-drachma coin. Take it and give it to them for my tax and yours" (17:27). Don't you think we'd be silly to interpret this as *the* way Jesus *always* wants Christians to pay their taxes?

> **Bible Fact**
>
> A commentary is a resource developed by a Bible scholar (or team of experts) in which the goal is to help Bible readers understand the meaning of Scripture. Some commentaries offer broad explanations of the entire Bible. Other commentaries seek to explain in great detail the contents of one particular Bible book.

- **Resist the urge to interpret Scripture on the basis of your own personal opinions, feelings, or experiences.** We all have built-in biases and presuppositions, but when we read the Bible, we want to be careful not to read *into* it. The big question isn't what do I *want* it to say and mean? It's what does it *actually* say and mean?

- **Remember that the Bible is all about Jesus.** He is the center of biblical revelation. The New Testament ingeniously shows how much the Old Testament pointed to Christ.

APPLY

Applying the Bible is moving from merely hearing the Word to doing what it says (James 1:22). Applying the Bible is taking action. It's living out God's truth. Here are some tips for being a doer of God's Word:

- **Ask yourself**, *What is the timeless principle or truth I gleaned from the Engage step of my reading?* For example, in the passage just

cited (Matthew 17:27), a bad interpretation would be that at tax time I need to go fishing. A better interpretation would be that Christ's followers should submit to proper authorities.

■ **Assess how your own current life situation mirrors** or dovetails with the truth of what you've just read. Maybe tax season is coming up. Maybe the law says you're supposed to get a city construction permit for that remodeling project you're about to do in your hall bath, but most people don't; and you'd rather skip the hassle and save the $45 permit fee, so . . .

■ **Ask these other application questions of your passage:**

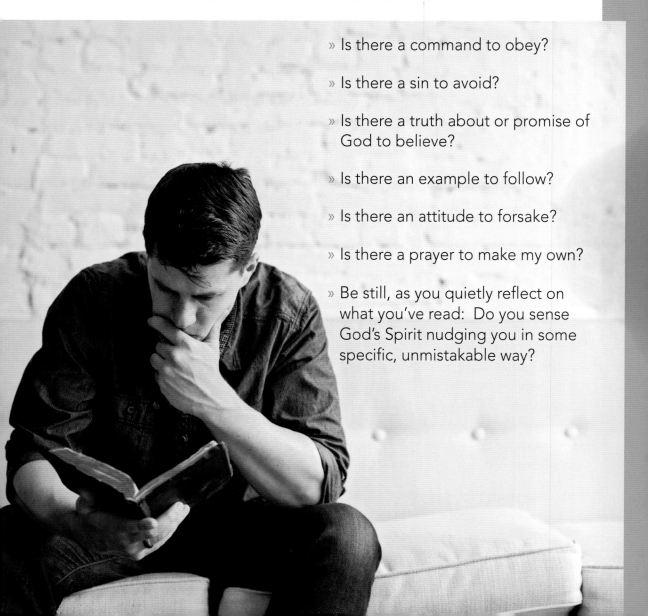

» Is there a command to obey?

» Is there a sin to avoid?

» Is there a truth about or promise of God to believe?

» Is there an example to follow?

» Is there an attitude to forsake?

» Is there a prayer to make my own?

» Be still, as you quietly reflect on what you've read: Do you sense God's Spirit nudging you in some specific, unmistakable way?

FAQ ABOUT READING THE BIBLE

When should I read?

Read when you're most alert and least distracted. Read when you won't be in a rush.

How much should I read at once?

Always try to read a "unit of thought" in its entirety. In a book like Proverbs, a distinct unit of thought might be just a verse or two. In a book like Psalms, it'll be an entire psalm/chapter. In a short book like 2 John, it'll be the whole book— really not much longer than a postcard. In the Gospels—Matthew, Mark, Luke, and John—it'll be a stand-alone parable told by Jesus or a story of him doing a miracle. Most times, chapter breaks are good stopping points. Just know that sometimes these chapter breaks (added to the Bible in the fifteenth century) interrupt the author's flow of thought, sort of like when your televised movie cuts in mid-scene to go to a commercial. Many Bibles today also include subheadings to help you know when a passage begins and ends.

How should I read?

Read prayerfully, carefully, humbly, curiously, and expectantly. If you are open to hearing from God, good things will come about!

5. Why are the different parts of the Bible so, well, different?

You don't have to be a Bible scholar to notice there's a difference between reading, say, 1 Samuel in the Old Testament and the apostle Paul's letter to the Romans in the New Testament.

To really "get" the Bible, we have to first realize, as mentioned earlier, that it's composed of different kinds of literature, or *genres*, interspersed throughout the Bible. Often books that comprise mostly a similar genre are grouped together in the Bible, but there are notable exceptions. Here's a good snapshot of the basic types of biblical content:

Genre	Definition	Percentage of Bible	Example
HISTORY/ NARRATIVES (including Law)	These are the stories where the action takes place—characters do things. (Note: The first five books of the Bible are viewed as books of history and books of law.)	60%	Genesis, Gospel of Matthew
PROPHECY	These writings record God's specific messages to his people through his prophets.	20%	Isaiah
EPISTLES	These are letters written either to individuals or groups of people.	7%	1 Corinthians
WISDOM	These writings give profound insight into God or the human condition.	6%	Proverbs
POETRY	These writings emphasize the human experience as we relate to God—these can be prayers, poems, and songs.	5%	Psalms, Song of Songs
APOCALYPTIC LITERATURE	These mysterious writings give us a peek into the end times.	2%	Daniel, Revelation

Old Testament

HISTORY/NARRATIVES

What to Know: About 40 percent of the Old Testament texts are stories—historical records of how God interacted with people. Like every good story, each one has characters who want something and face obstacles.

Where to Find: Many Old Testament stories—like Moses and the parting of the Red Sea or David defeating Goliath—are found in the books of Genesis through Esther. There are also narratives about the lives of the prophets in books like Daniel and Jonah.

How to Read:

- Always try to get a sense of the context. For example, ask, What has led up to this? Where does this take place?

- Keep in mind that like instruments in an orchestra, each small story adds something to the overall story God is telling.

- Pay attention to dialogue, so you know who the speakers are, and look for repeated words or phrases to help you understand important details.

- Remember that despite many differences between Old Testament characters and us, we share many of the same human emotions, struggles, and experiences.

- Don't expect to find a line at the end of each story that says "The moral of the story is . . . " Usually, a story's main message is indirect. Prayerfully ask God, "What are you saying through this story?"

LAW

What to Know: The law is a reflection of God's holy character. It also illustrates how the people of God are called to live holy lives. It came to Israel as a covenant, like a binding treaty.

Exhibit Hall 1

Where to Find: The law is concentrated in the books of Genesis through Deuteronomy, but discussions of God's laws are located in many places throughout the Old Testament. (The first five books of the Bible include many stories, making them also narrative literature.)

How to Read:

- Remember that *law* means instruction; God shows us his goodness by giving us instructions for how to live.

- If you begin to feel overwhelmed when reading the Old Testament laws, don't despair. Spoiler alert: The New Testament points out that the law was never meant to be a ladder to God. Rather, it was given to show us our need for God. Jesus is the only person who ever kept the law perfectly. In fact, it all points to him!

- Recognize that each law or commandment says something about God, his character, and his expectations—or about our own nature.

- Look for differences and similarities between the ancient Israelites and us. Even with a different context, God remains the same.

- Remember that Jesus summarized the law as loving God whole-heartedly and loving others unselfishly.

POETRY

What to Know: Poetry in the Bible is beautiful, emotional, image-rich expressions of the human condition. The psalms (150 in all) have various purposes: to lament, celebrate, express thanksgiving, offer praise, rejoice in God's salvation, record history, provide wisdom, and curse evil.

Where to Find: Psalms, Song of Songs, and some of the wisdom books are teeming with poetry. You'll also find poems scattered within various Old Testament stories.

How to Read:

- Don't expect Hebrew poetry to rhyme! It depends more on repetition and alliteration.

- Look for reoccurring words and phrases.

- See if you can detect the theme or main idea of the writer.

- Appreciate how emotional and raw and authentic the poems are. (This is a very different kind of faith expression than most first-time Bible readers expect!)

- Make the Bible's poems your own prayers to God.

WISDOM

What to Know: Wisdom literature typically focuses on God and the human experience. Wisdom literature is often written in the format of poetry.

Where to Find: Job, Proverbs, and Ecclesiastes are known as wisdom books—but of course there are wise words throughout the Bible!

How to Read:

- Understand that the proverbs are not promises. They offer widely observed, generally true principles of life. Remember that just because the Bible *reports* certain truths (for example, Proverbs 17:8 records that bribes are often effective), that doesn't mean it *endorses* such things.

- Note how concise and memorable the proverbs are. You might wish to memorize certain favorite ones. Think of Jesus as the fulfillment of wisdom. Ask, How might Jesus illustrate the ultimate wisdom of this proverb or statement?

- Pray for God to grant you insight. He is the source and giver of wisdom.

PROPHECY

What to Know: Prophetic literature includes words or messages from God via prophets or prophetesses about issues such as the condition of the people's hearts, the nature of God, repentance, obedience to God, judgments, blessings, victories, salvation, and woes.

Where to Find: The Old Testament prophecy books are Isaiah through Malachi, but you'll also find messages from prophets within many Old Testament stories.

How to Read:

- Note that the prophets typically show up in Scripture when people or nations have turned to false gods.

- Know that prophetic books are collections of individual revelations called oracles.

- Read each prophetic book within the author's own historical context—this is a must.

- Realize that the Bible contains prophetic warnings against nations opposed to God and his people, but the majority of the prophetic writings in Scripture are aimed at the people of God.

- When you read a prophecy that refers to an upcoming event, investigate further by asking, Was this fulfilled in the Old Testament or through Jesus? Or are we still awaiting its fulfillment?

HISTORY/NARRATIVES

What to Know: The Gospels (Matthew, Mark, Luke, and John) are narrative accounts that provide portraits of Jesus. They complement and inform one another. The Gospels tell us about the birth and life of Christ, whereas Acts tells us about the birth and life of Christ's church. Together they comprise 60 percent of the New Testament.

Where to Find: The first five books of the New Testament—Matthew through Acts—are history/narrative books.

How to Read:

- Realize that each Gospel writer had a different emphasis and audience: Matthew wrote primarily to Jews about Jesus being the Messiah. This is why he frequently quotes the Old Testament. Mark wrote to a Roman audience about Christ's servant nature. Notice how action-oriented his short book is. Luke wrote to Greeks and emphasized Jesus' perfect humanity. John's Gospel was written to prove that Jesus is the Christ, the Son of God, and to urge readers to believe in Christ.

- Recognize that Acts, also written by Luke, traces the growth of Jesus' church and the Spirit-led advance of Jesus' gospel from Jerusalem to Judea to Samaria—all the way "to the ends of the earth" (Acts 1:8).

EPISTLES

What to Know: Church leaders (primarily Paul) wrote these letters to various churches and individuals. We accept them as authoritative for teaching and living.

Where to Find: The New Testament epistles consist of thirteen letters by Paul (Romans through Philemon) plus eight other letters (Hebrews through Jude).

How to Read:

- Note that the book of Acts sheds light on the historical context and background of Paul's letters.

- Realize that these letters resulted from specific questions and problems their recipients faced.

- Notice that Paul liked to begin his letters with reminders of what we *believe*. He liked to end his letters with very practical reminders of how to *behave* (for example, Ephesians, Colossians, Romans).

- Look for common themes: worship, relationships, false teachers, living purely in an impure world.

- Look beyond the specific incident to the general principle. For example, Paul's discussion of eating meat in 1 Corinthians 8 is really about being mindful of others.

APOCALYPTIC LITERATURE

What to Know: Our word *apocalyptic* comes from a Greek word that means "to reveal." The emphasis in this kind of literature is on God's eventual salvation of his people and punishment of the wicked.

Where to Find: The Bible's primary apocalyptic book is the book of Revelation, though other books also contain end-time references: 1 and 2 Thessalonians and Matthew in the New Testament; and Isaiah, Joel, Zechariah, and Daniel in the Old Testament.

How to Read:

- Realize that the apostle John wrote Revelation after God gave him an epic vision of the end of the world at the end of his life.

- Recognize the marks of apocalyptic literature: good versus evil; angels and demons; and a focus on the Messiah (Jesus).

- Note that Revelation uses symbols—animals, colors, numbers, and cataclysmic imagery—to point to things that are real but not in a literal way. For example, the "beast" in Revelation 11:7 is an evil person, not an animal.

- Remember that Revelation reveals certain events at the end of the age but does not give an exact time line. Its ultimate purpose is to assure readers that God wins and that he will one day make "all things new" (21:5 NASB).

Now that you have a broad overview of the Bible as God's Word, maybe you'd like to get a better understanding of Bible geography. That's what we'll explore in chapter (or exhibit hall) 2.

Chapter 2

GETTING YOUR BEARINGS: BASIC BIBLE GEOGRAPHY

Exhibit Hall 5
Exploring the Content:
A Breakdown of Bible Books

Exhibit Hall 7
Connecting the Dots:
Jesus throughout the Bible

Exhibit Hall 4
Meeting the Characters:
A Who's Who of Bible People

Exhibit Hall 8
Peeking into the Future:
Heaven, Hell, and Eternity

Exhibit Hall 6
Getting to the Heart of the Bible:
Jesus' Life and Teachings

Exhibit Hall 3
Grasping the Story:
A Time Line of Bible History

Exhibit Hall 9
Summarizing the Message:
Major Themes in the Bible

Exhibit Hall 2
Getting Your Bearings:
Basic Bible Geography
You are here.

Exhibit Hall 1
Diving In:
A Quick Overview of the Bible

In one way, paper maps are going the way of the dodo bird. Few people pick up maps anymore—at least to navigate roads. Thanks to GPS technology and a host of apps, you can program your phone to give you voice-command directions to almost anywhere.

But if you want to *investigate* a place—if you want to get your bearings, get a better sense of where, say, the Grand Canyon is in relation to the Rocky Mountains—a map is the way to go.

Here in chapter two of your self-guided tour of God's Word, the goal is to get you oriented. In this exhibit hall, you'll find key geographical sites—like cities, mountains, rivers, and deserts—mentioned in the Bible. By getting a 30,000-foot view of the *places* in Scripture, you'll be able to better connect the *stories and events* of Scripture.

We'll begin where the Bible begins: in Mesopotamia.

Mesopotamia

About

The region of Mesopotamia (from the Greek word meaning "between the rivers") roughly corresponds to modern-day Iraq, along with portions of Iran, Syria, and Turkey. The Garden of Eden (Genesis 1–3) was located here, somewhere between the Tigris and Euphrates Rivers. Mostly dry and arid, this area features mild winters and hot summers. In some Bible translations, it is called Shinar (Daniel 1:2) or Chaldea (Jeremiah 50:10).

What Happened Here

- Adam and Eve rebelled against God (Genesis 3).
- Noah's ark—after the great flood—came to rest somewhere on the Ararat mountain range (Genesis 6–9).
- The tower of Babel was built here (Genesis 11).
- The Sumerians invented the first writing here (c. 3200 BC).
- Abraham (a.k.a. Abram) was originally from this region: "Ur of the Chaldeans" (Genesis 11:31); "Mesopotamia" (Acts 7:2).
- Hammurabi became the king of Babylon (c. 1792 BC).
- This region served as the headquarters for the Babylonian Empire. It's where King Nebuchadnezzar took God's people into captivity and where the prophet Daniel ministered.

Biblical Significance

- From a biblical perspective, Mesopotamia is the cradle of humanity and the setting for the first twelve chapters of the Bible.

- The Magi ("wise men") of the Christmas story are believed to have been from Mesopotamia (Matthew 2:1).

- Some of the visitors to Jerusalem at Pentecost were also from here (Acts 2:9).

> **Factoid**
>
> We owe our sixty-second minute and sixty-minute hour to the Sumerian culture of ancient Mesopotamia.

"Terah took his son Abram, his grandson Lot son of Haran, and his daughter-in-law Sarai, the wife of his son Abram, and together they set out from Ur of the Chaldeans to go to Canaan." —Genesis 11:31

Great Ancient Empires at a Glance

Empire	Dates	Key Leaders
Sumerian	3200–1900 BC	Gilgamesh
Egyptian	2700–1100 BC	Cheops, Ramses II
Akkadian	2300–2150 BC	Sargon
Babylonian	1790–1590 BC	Hammurabi
Hittite	1400–1200 BC	Suppiluliuma I, Mursilli II
Assyrian	1350–609 BC	Ashurbanipal
Israel	1051–586 BC	Saul, David, Solomon
Neo-Babylonian	626–539 BC	Nebuchadnezzar
Persian	539–323 BC	Cyrus the Great, Darius

(Dates are approximate and reflect the period that the empires were at their height.)

Now let's head quite a bit west and a little south to the land of Egypt.

Mediterranean
Sea

Sidon
Damascus
Tyre
▲ Mt. Hermon
Ptolemais
Hazor
Sea of Galilee
Mt. Carmel
Ain
Megiddo
Mt. Gilboa ▲
Caesarea
Samaria
Jordan River
PHILISTIA
Mt. Ebal ▲
Joppa
Mt.
Gerizim ▲ Shiloh
Bethel
Gilgal
Amman
CANAAN
Gezer
AMMON
Ashdod
Jerusalem
Jericho
Ashkelon
Bethlehem
Mt. Nebo ▲
JUDAH
Hebron
Dead Sea
Ziph
En-Gedi
MOAB
Gaza
Beersheba
Arad
NEGEV
EDOM
Etham
Migdol
GOSHEN
Desert
of Shur
AMALEK
Ramesses
Succoth?
Kadesh-barnea
Pithom
Desert
of Zin
Desert
of Paran
Makheloth?
On
Timnah
Noph
(Memphis)
Abronah
Ezion-Geber
EGYPT
SINAI
Jotbathah
Desert
of Sin
Nile River
Nuweiba
Marah
Dophkah
Hazeroth
Elim
Rephidim
Paran
Di-zahab
Desert
of Sinai
MIDIAN

▲ Mt. Sinai?

©Michael Schmeling, www.aridocean.com

Red Sea

Egypt

About

Often referred to as the "gift of the Nile," Egypt is a country situated in far northeast Africa. Today, at 387,000 square miles (1,002,325 sq km), Egypt is almost one and a half times the size of Texas. It is one of the oldest civilizations in the world and in ancient times (4000–2000 BC) was highly advanced, developing numbering systems and the science of astronomy, and building libraries. The Egyptians were polytheistic (worshiped many gods) during Old Testament times before the initial spread of Christianity in the first century AD. Since the seventh century its people have been predominantly devoted to Islam.

What Happened Here

- The 365-day calendar was introduced (2772 BC).
- The pyramids were built (2700–2200 BC).
- Papyrus, a plant, was first used to make paper (starting 3000 BC).
- Abraham lived for a time in Egypt (Genesis 12:10).
- Joseph, the son of Jacob, was sold to slave traders who took him to Egypt (Genesis 37:28–36). God used this event to prepare the way for all of Abraham's descendants to end up in Egypt.

- After 400 years in Egypt (much of that time as slaves), the Israelites were led by Moses to freedom through the Red Sea to the east, and into the desert wilderness south of Canaan—the land God promised to Abraham. In liberating his chosen people, God also brought judgment on Egypt (Exodus 7–12).

- Joseph and Mary fled to Egypt with the infant Jesus to escape King Herod's murderous decree (Matthew 2:13–18).

Biblical Significance

- Because of the fertile soil in the Nile delta, Egypt was the breadbasket to the ancient world. In this sense, it sometimes provided a refuge for the people of God. However, since it was also a place of oppression and polytheistic worship, it represented danger for the people of God.

Factoid

The Egyptians wrote first in hieroglyphics, a kind of picture language. In time this was mixed with a popular cursive script. The discovery of the Rosetta Stone in AD 1799 provided a key by which this ancient language could be interpreted.

- Historically, Egypt is where the people of God found themselves in literal, physical bondage as slaves. Following their deliverance by God, some of the Israelites were afraid and discussed going "back to Egypt" (Numbers 14:3). This became a spiritual metaphor for refusing to trust God and turning back to an old way of life.

> **"I am the LORD your God, who brought you out of Egypt so that you would no longer be slaves to the Egyptians."**
> **—Leviticus 26:13**

Our next stop is the Promised Land. Because of the area's geographical diversity, we'll look at it in two parts: first northern Israel and then southern Israel.

Sidon

Damascus

Zarephath

Mt. Hermon ▲

SYRIA

Tyre

Dan

Caesarea-Philippi

TETRARCHY
OF PHILIP

*Mediterranean
Sea*

Ptolemais
(Acco)

Chorazin

Seleucia

Bethsaida

Naveh

Capernaum

*Sea of
Galilee*

Mt. Carmel ▲

Cana

Dion

Nazareth

GALILEE

Gadara

Abilene

Megiddo

Mt. Gilboa ▲

DECAPOLIS

Caesarea

Samaria

SAMARIA

Gerasa

Shechem

Mt. Ebal ▲

Mt. Gerizim ▲

Sychar

Jordan River

Joppa

Antipatris

PEREA

Ephraim

Jamnia

Emmaus

Jericho

Mt. Nebo ▲

Ashdod

Qumran

Jerusalem

Bethany

Ashkelon

JUDEA

Bethlehem

*Wilderness
of Judea*

*Dead
Sea*

Gaza

Hebron

En-Gedi

IDUMEA

Masada

Beersheba

©Michael Schmeling, www.aridocean.com

Northern Israel

About

Israel is bound on the west by the Mediterranean Sea and roughly on the east by three bodies of water: the Sea of Galilee, the Jordan River, and the Dead Sea.

The northern part of Israel is about the geographical size of New Jersey. This region (which includes Galilee and Samaria) offers a diverse climate and varied landscape. The landscape is lush with vegetation, far different from the arid and hostile regions to the south.

What Happened Here

- In the Old Testament, the prophet Elijah confronted 850 false prophets at Mount Carmel (1 Kings 18:16–40).

- Hosea the prophet warned the inhabitants of northern Israel to turn back to God. This was around 750 BC, the same time as the founding of Rome, some 1,300 miles (2,092 km) west.

- The northern kingdom of Israel fell to the invading Assyrian army in 722 BC. When the Assyrians resettled foreigners in this conquered area, the Jews still residing there intermarried with them, producing the people known as the Samaritans.

- Jesus grew up in Nazareth, a town in northern Israel.

- Jesus ministered in Galilee, exactly where the prophet Isaiah said the Messiah would be "a great light" to the people there (Isaiah 9:1–2; Matthew 4:13–16). Jesus taught the masses in this region and miraculously fed over 5,000 people with a boy's lunch (Mark 6:33–44). He calmed a storm on the Sea of Galilee (Mark 4:35–41) and walked on its waves (Mark 6:45–52).

Names for Israel

In the Bible and in history, the land of Israel (in part and/or in whole) has been referred to by many names:

- Canaan (Exodus 6:4)
- The Promised Land (Deuteronomy 6:3)
- Judah (southern part) and Israel (northern part)
- The Holy Land (Psalm 78:54)
- Palestine

Biblical Significance

- When Jesus began his public ministry, he went to the local synagogue meeting in Nazareth and read an explicit prophecy about the coming Messiah from the book of Isaiah; he then said, "Today this scripture is fulfilled in your hearing" (Luke 4:21). This is *the* big question of the Bible: Is Jesus who he claimed to be? And if so, how will we respond?

> **"Philip found Nathanael and told him, 'We have found the one Moses wrote about in the Law, and about whom the prophets also wrote—Jesus of Nazareth, the son of Joseph.'" —John 1:45**

Now we'll head a few miles south to southern Israel. Watch how much conditions change over such a short distance.

Factoid

Mount Hermon in northern Israel gets enough snow in the winter months to accommodate skiers and snowboarders. (As far as we know, no Bible characters ever skied in the snow here.)

View from the Jumping Mountain in Nazareth

Place	Elevation	Average January Temperature (highs to lows)	Average July Temperature (highs to lows)	Average Annual Rainfall
Nineveh (in ancient Mesopotamia), near modern-day Mosul, Iraq	732 feet (223 m)	54–36°F (12.4–2.2°C)	109–77°F (42.9–25°C)	14.3 inches (363.6 mm)
Cairo, Egypt	75 feet (23 m)	66–48°F (18.9–9°C)	94–72°F (34.7–20.1°C)	.97 inches (24.7 mm)
Nazareth, Israel (northern Israel)	1,138 feet (347 m)	59–44°F (15–7°C)	88–69°F (31–21°C)	22.8 inches (580 mm)
Jerusalem, Israel (southern Israel)	2,474 feet (754 m)	53–43°F (12–9°C)	84–67°F (29–19°C)	21.8 inches (554.1 mm)
Iconium, Turkey (ancient Asia Minor), now called Konya	3,900 feet (1,200 m)	40–25°F (4.8–3.9°C)	86–61°F (30.2–16.1°C)	12.6 inches (319.7 mm)
Rome, Italy	69 feet (21 m)	53–37°F (12–3°C)	86–64°F (30–18°C)	31.66 inches (804.3 mm)
Sea of Galilee (Tiberias, on the western shore)	–696 feet (–212 m)	65–49°F (18–10°C)	100–73°F (38–23°C)	17 inches (431.8 mm)
Mount Nebo (in modern-day Jordan)	2,680 feet (817 m)	54–38°F (12.3–3.6°C)	89–65°F (32–18.5°C)	10.6 inches (269.2 mm)
Judean Desert (Kalya, by the Dead Sea)	–1,181 feet (–360 m)	68–53°F (20–11°C)	102–83°F (38–28°C)	2 inches (50.8 mm)

Exhibit Hall 2

Exhibit Hall 2

Southern Israel

About

The southern region of Israel is roughly the area west and south of the Dead Sea. Unlike northern Israel, which features snow-capped mountains, the southern region is dominated by the Negev, a desert of some 6,100 square miles (about 15,799 sq km).

Jordan River

What Happened Here

- In 1406 BC the twelve tribes of Israel, under Joshua's leadership, invaded Canaan at Jericho. Three of the tribes settled southern Israel: Judah, the largest of the twelve tribes; Benjamin; and Simeon, the smallest.

- After the reign of King Solomon, the kingdom of Israel split (931 BC). The two large tribes in the south (Benjamin and Judah) took the name of the larger tribe, "Judah." The other tribes in the north took the name "Israel."

- The people of Judah were taken captive by the Babylonians (605–586 BC).

- Though Jesus spent most of his life in northern Israel, key events from his life—his birth, baptism, crucifixion, burial, resurrection, and ascension—happened in southern Israel, mostly in and around Jerusalem.

Biblical Significance

- The story of Mary and Joseph connects northern and southern Israel. Commanded to return to his hometown for a Roman census, Joseph took his pregnant wife and left their home in Nazareth, in the lush green north, and headed south to Bethlehem, with its more arid environment. This 80-mile (129 km) trip is a four- to five-day walk.

Mary and Joseph may have followed the Jewish tradition of skirting Samaria on the east, going along the lush Jordan Valley and going through the historic city of Jericho.

> **Factoid**
>
> Jerusalem is on the same latitude as El Paso, Texas.

From Jericho, which lies at an extremely low elevation, travelers must endure a steep climb to reach Jerusalem. The ascent rises about 3,500 feet (1,067 mm). This would be exhausting for anyone and would have been even more so for a woman in the latter part of her pregnancy. It is likely that from here, Mary and Joseph would have headed farther south to Bethlehem. Here, Jesus was born (Luke 2:1–21).

■ The prophet Zechariah foretold about a significant event occurring in this region: "On that day his feet will stand on the Mount of Olives, east of Jerusalem, and the Mount of Olives will be split in two from east to west, forming a great valley, with half of the mountain moving north and half moving south" (Zechariah 14:4).

"But you, Bethlehem, in the land of Judah, are by no means least among the rulers of Judah; for out of you will come a ruler who will shepherd my people Israel."
—Matthew 2:6

Next, let's zero in on Jerusalem, the geographical epicenter of the biblical narrative.

Negev Desert

45

Jerusalem

About

One of the oldest cities in the world, Jerusalem is located in the center of southern Israel, some 15 miles (24 km) west of the Dead Sea and about 33 miles (53 km) east of the Mediterranean. Judaism, Christianity, and Islam all regard Jerusalem as a holy city.

What Happened Here

- On Mount Moriah in Jerusalem, Abraham offered back to God his beloved son Isaac (Genesis 22:1–19).
- King David established Jerusalem as the royal city of the Israelites (1 Chronicles 11:4–8).
- David's son Solomon built the temple on Mount Moriah (1 Kings 6–8).
- The Babylonians destroyed the temple and burned the city (2 Kings 25:9–10).
- The Jews returning from exile rebuilt the temple under Zerubbabel and then the walls of Jerusalem under Nehemiah (Ezra 1–6; Nehemiah 2–6).
- Jesus Christ was crucified, buried, and resurrected in Jerusalem.
- To quell an uprising, the Romans slaughtered many people in Jerusalem and destroyed the temple (AD 70). The temple has never been rebuilt.
- Muslims claim Muhammad made a miraculous, nocturnal visit to Jerusalem and then was transported to heaven before returning home (c. AD 620).

Biblical Significance

- Jerusalem was known as Jebus until the time of King David, and "the City of David" ever since (1 Chronicles 11:7). It is a key locale in the Bible, mentioned more than 800 times from the book of Joshua through the book of Revelation.
- About six weeks after the resurrection, God poured out his Holy Spirit on the disciples of Jesus who were gathered in Jerusalem to celebrate the Jewish festival of Pentecost (Acts 2). This marks the beginning of the church. If you are a follower of Jesus, your spiritual roots are truly found in the city of David!

Jesus said: "Jerusalem, Jerusalem, you who kill the prophets and stone those sent to you, how often I have longed to gather your children together, as a hen gathers her chicks under her wings, and you were not willing."
—Luke 13:34

Jerusalem with the Temple Mount and the gold Dome of the Rock (center)

Factoid

It's been estimated that the ancient city of Jerusalem has been destroyed twice, attacked more than fifty times, and captured and recaptured more than forty times.

The next stops on our self-guided tour look at some of the regions Jesus' disciples traveled to with the message of the gospel: Asia Minor, Greece, and Rome.

Sinope

CAPPADOCIA
Samosata
Caesarea
Ancyra
GALATIA
Aleppo
SYRIA
Hamath
Damascus
Petra
ARABIA
(PETRAEA)

BITHYNIA
AND PONTUS

Heraclea

Nicomedia

Byzantium

Black Sea

LYCAONIA
Iconium
CILICIA
Tarsus
Antioch
Tripolis
Tyre
Jerusalem

Lystra
PAMPHYLIA
CYPRUS
Pelusium

Colossae
Laodicea
Philadelphia
Thyatira
ASIA MINOR
Sardis
LYDIA
Patara
Rhodes

EGYPT
Memphis

Alexandria

Ephesus

Pergamum
Smyrna

Island
of Patmos

CRETE

THRACE
Philippi

Aegean
Sea

Athens

Mediterranean Sea

CYRENAICA

Thessalonica

Berea
GREECE
EPIRUS
Delphi
Corinth
Sparta
ACHAIA

Cyrene

MACEDONIA

Rhegium

Syracuse

SICILY

ILLYRICUM
(DALMATIA)

Adriatic
Sea

Cannae
Mt. Vesuvius

Ancona

Neapolis
ITALY

Rome

Tyrrhenian
Sea

TRIPOLITANIA

©Michael Schmeling, www.aridocean.com

Asia Minor

About

"Asia" in the New Testament typically refers to what we know today as western Turkey. The entire area often labeled "Asia Minor" on our maps was comprised in New Testament times of Asia, Galatia, Cappadocia, and various smaller provinces. Straddling Asia and Europe, Asia Minor is hemmed in by the Black Sea to the north, the Aegean Sea to the west, and the Mediterranean to the south. Eastern Turkey is mountainous and the site of Mount Ararat, where Noah's ark came to rest after the great flood.

Celsus Library in Ephesus, Turkey

What Happened Here

- The apostle Paul traveled through Asia, preaching the gospel on each of his three missionary journeys recorded in the book of Acts.

- Many churches sprang up across this region. Some received inspired letters from the apostle Paul (Ephesus, Colossae, Galatia).

- The seven churches mentioned by the apostle John in the book of Revelation are in Asia Minor: Ephesus, Smyrna, Pergamum, Thyatira, Sardis, Philadelphia, and Laodicea.

Biblical Significance

- About the same time the Romans were using soap in their elaborate public bathhouses (c. AD 50), Paul was talking to the residents of Asia about being washed spiritually by Christ (Ephesians 5:26).

- The city of Ephesus exemplified the decadent culture of Asia Minor, being full of brothels and famous for cult prostitution at the temple of the Roman goddess Diana (known to the Greeks as Artemis). This was a challenging place for new Christians to live without falling back into old lifestyles.

Paul's ministry in Ephesus "went on for two years, so that all the Jews and Greeks who lived in the province of Asia heard the word of the Lord." —Acts 19:10

Factoid

Ankara, Turkey, is on the same latitude as Beijing, China, and Philadelphia, Pennsylvania.

Exhibit Hall 2

Greece and Rome

About

Often called the birthplace of Western civilization, Greece is located in southeastern Europe. With its thousands of islands, it extends into the Mediterranean and Aegean Seas, making it a popular destination for modern-day tourists. In the first century, it was a bustling center of commerce and culture.

Rome, some 650 miles (1,046 km) northwest of Athens, was the capital of the Roman Empire and one of the most influential cities on earth. It was an architectural marvel and a hotbed of religious paganism.

What Happened Here

- After being prevented on his second missionary journey from ministering further in Asia, Paul and his entourage received a vision from God directing Paul to head to Macedonia (Acts 16:6–9). This led to Paul's extensive ministry in Greece, either starting or strengthening churches in Philippi, Thessalonica, Berea, and Corinth.

The Roman Forum, the center of civic life in ancient Rome

- At the end of his second trip, Paul wrote a long letter to the church at Rome and expressed his desire to visit. (This is the book of Romans in our Bibles today.)

- On his third missionary journey, Paul revisited many of the churches of Macedonia and Greece.

- Paul was arrested in Jerusalem and eventually taken to Rome. It's believed that both Paul and Peter were martyred near Rome in the AD 60s during Emperor Nero's brutal persecution of Christians.

Biblical Significance

- The Gospel of Mark—with its emphasis on action, servanthood, and Christ's power—was written to appeal to Roman readers (many of whom were slaves). The Gospel of Luke, with its focus on Christ's perfect humanity, was written to appeal to Greeks, who prized ideal manhood.

> **Factoid**
> At the time of the apostle Paul, about 25 percent of the people in the world lived and died under Roman law.

- The apostle Paul shared the gospel (literally "good news") of Jesus with everyone he encountered—rich, poor, Jew, Gentile, male, female, slave, or free (Galatians 3:28). However, as a smart, educated man, Paul relished the opportunity to talk with people in cities that wielded great influence.

"I am so eager to preach the gospel also to you who are in Rome." —Romans 1:15

Areopagus (Mars Hill), the site of Paul's famous sermon in Athens (Acts 17)

Let's shift our focus now from *where* (specific cities and countries) to *what* (special kinds of geography: bodies of water, mountains, and deserts).

Rose Publishing, Inc.   May be reproduced for classroom use only, not for sale.

51

Bodies of Water

About

Though certain locations in the Middle East are lush and green, much of this part of the world is dry. Little rainfall means a shortage of waterways and large lakes. Wadis (dry ravines) that dot the landscape contain water only during the brief rainy seasons.

Body of Water	Description	Key Events
Tigris River	From the Taurus Mountains in Turkey, the Tigris flows 1,150 miles (1,851 km) southeast through Syria and Iraq, past Baghdad to the Persian Gulf.	Abraham followed God's call via the Fertile Crescent, the region between the Tigris and Euphrates Rivers (Genesis 12).
Euphrates River	This river flows through the same countries as the Tigris for 1,740 miles (2,800 km), merging with the Tigris just northwest of the Persian Gulf.	The ancient cities of Ur and Babylon were located along the Euphrates River (Jeremiah 51:63–64).
Nile River	The longest river in the world (4,258 miles; 6,853 km), the Nile flows north, refreshing almost a dozen countries.	As a baby, Moses was placed in a basket in the Nile and the Nile figured prominently in God's judgments on Egypt (Exodus 2, 7–8).
Red Sea	Roughly 1,400 miles long (2,253 km) by 200 miles wide (322 km) at its widest point, the Red Sea forms the eastern border of Egypt.	God delivered his people out of Egypt through the miraculous parting of the Red Sea (Exodus 13–15).
Sea of Galilee	The lowest freshwater lake on earth (about 700 feet, or 213 m, below sea level), this lake is roughly 68 square miles in area (176 sq km)—about the same size as Washington, DC.	It is the site of many events from the life of Jesus, including where he walked on water (Matthew 14). It is also called the Lake of Gennesaret or Sea of Tiberias (Luke 5:1; John 6:1).
Jordan River	Meandering from the Sea of Galilee some 220 miles (354 km) to the Dead Sea, the Jordan River forms the eastern boundary of Israel.	The twelve tribes entered the Promised Land through the miraculously parted Jordan River (Joshua 3). John baptized Jesus here (Matthew 3:13–17).

Body of Water	Description	Key Events
Dead Sea (Salt Sea)	This lake is 31 miles long by 9 miles wide (50 km by 14 km) and has no life—other than microorganisms—found in it. It is almost ten times as salty as the ocean, leading to it also being called the Salt Sea. Its surface is over 1,400 feet (427 m) below sea level.	David sought refuge here (1 Samuel 23:29). A Jewish religious sect from before and around the time of Jesus hid the now-famous Dead Sea Scrolls at Qumran, a settlement overlooking the water.
Mediterranean Sea	Also known as the Great Sea, the Mediterranean is bordered on the north by Europe; the east by Turkey, Syria, Lebanon, and Israel; and on the south by Africa.	Jonah fled from the call of God by sailing on this sea. Paul's missionary journeys meant he spent time sailing on these waters.

Biblical Significance

- Jesus' demonstrations of his power over nature—like when he calmed a raging storm on the Sea of Galilee—served as signs to confirm that he was truly the Son of God (Mark 4:35–41).

- *Thirst* is a great (and frequent) metaphor in Scripture, because of the scarcity of water in the Middle East (Psalm 42:2; John 4:13–14). Just as physically we cannot live without water, spiritually we cannot live without the living water that Christ offers (John 7:37).

Factoid

The Jordan River is only about 90 to 100 feet (27 to 30 m) across and rarely more than 10 feet (3 m) in depth.

Sea of Galilee

Mountains

About

In ancient times, people often viewed mountains, hills, or high places (with their nearness to the heavens) as optimal locations for encountering the gods. Indeed, people in the Bible often had significant spiritual encounters with God on various mountains.

Most of the mountains in Israel aren't grand peaks; their elevations rarely exceed 3,000 feet (.9 km).

Mountain	Location	Height	Key Events
Mount Ararat	Asia Minor (modern-day Turkey)	16,854 feet (5,137 m)	Where Noah's ark came to rest after the flood (Genesis 8:4).
Mount Sinai (Mount Horeb)	Sinai region, exact location unknown	Unknown	Where Moses encountered God—first, through a burning bush; and forty years later, when he received Israel's law and experienced God's glory (Exodus 3; 33:6, 19–33).
Mount Gerizim and Mount Ebal	Northern Israel/Samaria	Gerizim: 2,849 feet (868 m) Ebal: 3,084 feet (940 m)	Two ridges from which blessings and curses, respectively, were pronounced (Deuteronomy 11:29). Where the ancient Samaritans built a temple (Mount Gerizim), and considered sacred even in Jesus' time (John 4).
Mount Nebo	East of the Jordan River	2,680 feet (817 m)	Where God showed Moses the Promised Land before he died (Deuteronomy 34:1–5).
Mount Gilboa	Northern Israel	1,629 feet (497 m)	Where King Saul and his sons died in battle (1 Samuel 31:8).
Mount Carmel	Northern Israel coastal region	1,791 feet (546 m)	Where the prophet Elijah confronted and defeated the prophets of Baal and Asherah (1 Kings 18:16–40).
Mount Moriah	Jerusalem	Unknown	Where Abraham almost sacrificed his son Isaac (Genesis 22). Where Solomon's temple was located (2 Chronicles 3:1). Where the Islamic Dome of the Rock sits today.

Mountain	Location	Height	Key Events
Mount Hermon	Between present-day Syria and Lebanon	9,232 feet (2,814 m)	Possibly where Christ was transfigured (shone with glory; see Psalms 42:6; 133:3; Mark 9:1–9). Often covered with snow and now boasts a ski resort; highest mountain in the region.
Mount Zion	Eastern hill/ high spot in Jerusalem	2,510 feet (765 m)	Often used poetically to imply God's glory and favor (Psalm 48:11; Revelation 14:1).
Mount of Olives	Jerusalem	2,710 feet (826 m)	Favorite place for Jesus and his disciples to hang out (for example, Matthew 21:1; Luke 21:37). Where Jesus ascended to heaven (Acts 1:9-12).

Biblical Significance

- Mountains provide perspective and protection. No wonder the psalmist exclaimed, "As the mountains surround Jerusalem, so the Lord surrounds his people both now and forevermore" (Psalm 125:2).

- The majesty of a great peak reaching up to the skies points us to our Creator (Isaiah 2:2). Make the prayer of the pilgrims (as they approached Jerusalem) your own:

"I lift up my eyes to the mountains—where does my help come from?" —Psalm 121:1

After looking at *wet* places and *high* places, we now shift our focus to *dry* places.

Sinai, Egypt

Deserts

About

The deserts in the Bible are like deserts everywhere: arid, uninviting, and harsh. The Negev, for example, which covers more than half of present-day Israel, is a hostile environment with mountains, canyons, and craters. In some areas sand dunes approach 100 feet (30 m) in height. The Negev gets little rainfall (less than 10 inches, or 254 mm, annually) and subjects its inhabitants to temperatures that can top 100°F (37.8°C) in the summer. Temperatures in the winter months hover in the 40s–50s°F (5–15°C), dipping below freezing on occasion.

Factoid

At roughly 23,000 square miles (59,570 sq km), the Sinai Desert is almost the size of West Virginia.

Desert	Key Events
Desert of Shur	Where God told Hagar to return to Sarai (Sarah) (Genesis 16:7–9).
Desert of Paran	Ishmael's home when Hagar found him an Egyptian wife (Genesis 21:21).
Desert of Beersheba	Where Hagar went when Abraham sent her away (Genesis 21:14). Where Elijah retreated and wanted to die (1 Kings 19:3–4).
Desert of Sin	Where the Israelites complained and God provided manna and quail for them to eat (Exodus 16:1–31).
Desert of Sinai	Where God gave Moses the Ten Commandments (Exodus 19–20).
Desert of Zin	Where Moses' sister Miriam died (Numbers 20:1). Where God provided water from a rock (Numbers 27:14).
Desert of Ziph	A place where David hid from King Saul (1 Samuel 23:14–15).
Desert of En Gedi	Another place where David hid from King Saul (1 Samuel 24:1).
Desert of Edom	Where Israel and Judah fought Moab (2 Kings 3:6–8).
Wilderness of Judea	Where John the Baptist began his ministry (Matthew 3). Likely where Jesus spent forty days fasting (Matthew 4).

As inhospitable as this seems, Abraham spent considerable time here, and David retreated to the Negev when hiding from King Saul.

Biblical Significance

- After his baptism in the Jordan, Jesus entered the wilderness for forty days of testing (Matthew 3:13–4:11). Jesus succeeded where Israelites in the Old Testament did not: people went through the Red Sea and into the wilderness, where they failed to trust and obey God (Exodus 14–17). Jesus, however, showed himself to be the true servant of God.

- In the Bible, deserts are often the locales where the people of God endure trials and tests. Today our "desert" experiences may be metaphorical, but they still offer opportunities for us to trust God to supply the things our souls need.

> **"They did not thirst when he led them through the deserts; he made water flow for them from the rock; he split the rock and water gushed out." —Isaiah 48:21**

Now that you've got your bearings in Bible lands, let's move to the next exhibit hall where you'll get your bearings in Bible history with a bird's-eye view of the story of the Bible.

Judea Desert

GRASPING THE STORY: A TIME LINE OF BIBLE HISTORY

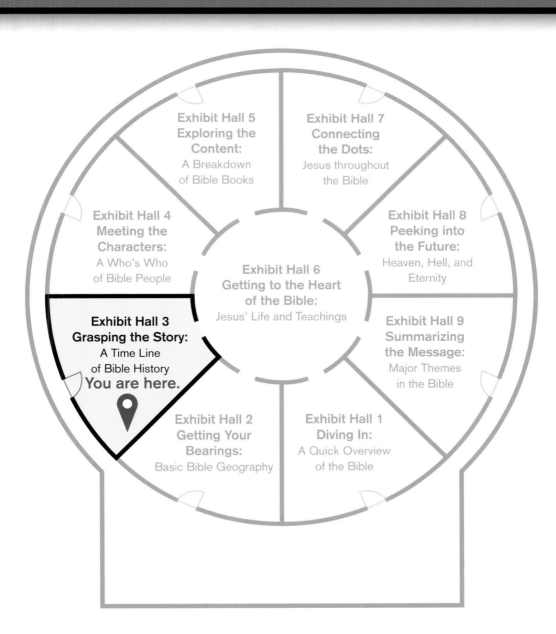

Exhibit Hall 5
Exploring the
Content:
A Breakdown
of Bible Books

Exhibit Hall 7
Connecting
the Dots:
Jesus throughout
the Bible

Exhibit Hall 4
Meeting the
Characters:
A Who's Who
of Bible People

Exhibit Hall 8
Peeking into
the Future:
Heaven, Hell, and
Eternity

Exhibit Hall 6
Getting to the Heart
of the Bible:
Jesus' Life and Teachings

Exhibit Hall 3
Grasping the Story:
A Time Line
of Bible History
You are here.

Exhibit Hall 9
Summarizing
the Message:
Major Themes
in the Bible

Exhibit Hall 2
Getting Your
Bearings:
Basic Bible Geography

Exhibit Hall 1
Diving In:
A Quick Overview
of the Bible

Some first-time readers of the Bible are surprised to discover that the Bible is more than a bunch of dos and don'ts.

Sure, it contains a lot of instructional material. And the Bible also includes poetic and prophetic writings. But mostly, the Bible contains narrative literature. A narrative is a story told to convey a message through people and their life situations and problems. A narrative is action: This happened, then this happened, then this happened . . .

The bottom line? The Bible is mostly story. In fact, it's one big story made up of lots of smaller stories. In truth, the Bible is *God's* story. It's the real, true story of the world—and it's *our* story. Or we could say it's the story of how God created, sustains, and interacts with the people he made.

Here's why that matters: Once we really understand the implications of *this* story, our lives are never the same.

In this *Self-Guided Tour of the Bible*, we're imagining the Bible as a vast museum, with nine separate exhibit halls worth our attention. Exhibit hall 1 (chapter 1) focuses on the Bible's claim to be the inspired, trustworthy revelation of God. Exhibit hall 2 (chapter 2) features a quick overview of basic Bible geography. It helps us get the lay of the land.

In this room (i.e., the next few pages), we want to get a solid understanding of the basic *story* of the Bible. What are the key historical events that happened and when did they occur? We'll look at a time line for all that, but first . . .

The Secret Few People Know

Most people get confused when they try to read straight through the Bible. That's because nobody ever told them one very important fact. Here it is: The story of the Bible doesn't begin in Genesis and then continue chronologically and sequentially through each of the sixty-six books all the way to the last page of the book of Revelation.

Actually, the essential story of the Bible is found in just twenty-two of the sixty-six Bible books—the history books. It makes sense that the *story* would be found in the *history* books, right?

It's when people grasp how the Bible is organized—into two *testaments* and assorted *categories*—that the lightbulbs really begin to click on.

Testament	Category	Books	Number of Books
OLD TESTAMENT	History (including Law)	From Genesis to Esther	17
	Poetry/Wisdom	From Job to Song of Songs	5
	Prophecy	From Isaiah to Malachi	17
NEW TESTAMENT	History	From Matthew to Acts	5
	Epistles (Letters)	From Romans to Jude	21
	Prophecy (Apocalyptic)	Revelation	1
		TOTAL	66

Exhibit Hall 3

The sixty-six books of the Bible are divided into the Old and New Testaments.

- The thirty-nine books of the Old Testament were the books written before Jesus' birth.

- The twenty-seven books of the New Testament were written after Jesus' birth.

These testaments (also known as covenants, or agreements) are more than historical time lines. They distinguish the way God interacts with his people.

- In the Old Testament, God is revealed through priests and prophets, and worship is experienced primarily within the temple. Each book looks forward to and points to a coming Messiah (Jesus).

- In the New Testament, access to God is made available to all through Jesus. The believer's heart becomes a temple and the place God resides.

This difference is important to keep in mind when reading books from either testament.

Add the seventeen Old Testament historical books to the five New Testament historical books (the four Gospels and the book of Acts), and you get twenty-two books of history. For the most part, that's where we read the basic story of the Bible.

So what's with the other forty-four books? All those books of poetry, wisdom, prophecy, and epistles? What purpose do they serve? They *supplement* the story and give us indispensable, behind-the-scenes details. They're inspired and of utmost importance. They make the story come alive and show (or suggest) human reactions to divine actions at various points *in* the story.

The following diagram shows how and where the other forty-four books fit into the Bible story told in the twenty-two historical books. Take a close look at the diagram.

Do you see it? If you simply want to understand the basic story of the Bible, the twenty-two history books in the column on the left will give it to you.

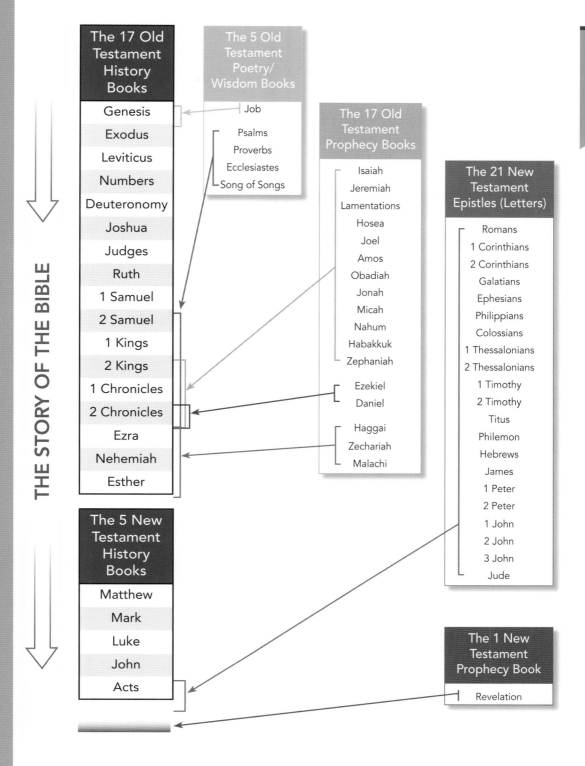

THE STORY OF THE BIBLE

The 17 Old Testament History Books

Genesis
Exodus
Leviticus
Numbers
Deuteronomy
Joshua
Judges
Ruth
1 Samuel
2 Samuel
1 Kings
2 Kings
1 Chronicles
2 Chronicles
Ezra
Nehemiah
Esther

The 5 Old Testament Poetry/ Wisdom Books

Job
Psalms
Proverbs
Ecclesiastes
Song of Songs

The 17 Old Testament Prophecy Books

Isaiah
Jeremiah
Lamentations
Hosea
Joel
Amos
Obadiah
Jonah
Micah
Nahum
Habakkuk
Zephaniah
Ezekiel
Daniel
Haggai
Zechariah
Malachi

The 21 New Testament Epistles (Letters)

Romans
1 Corinthians
2 Corinthians
Galatians
Ephesians
Philippians
Colossians
1 Thessalonians
2 Thessalonians
1 Timothy
2 Timothy
Titus
Philemon
Hebrews
James
1 Peter
2 Peter
1 John
2 John
3 John
Jude

The 5 New Testament History Books

Matthew
Mark
Luke
John
Acts

The 1 New Testament Prophecy Book

Revelation

To use a travel metaphor, think of the twenty-two history books as the express lane through the Bible. Think of the other forty-four books as interesting byways and scenic loops to off-the-beaten-track sites and not-to-be-missed attractions. They add color, beauty, and "wow!" moments to your trip.

Okay, now that you have a better sense of *how* the different books fit together and *where* the story of the Bible is found, *what* exactly is that story? Great question!

"For everything that was written in the past was written to teach us, so that through the endurance taught in the Scriptures and the encouragement they provide we might have hope." — Romans 15:4

Direct Route

Scenic Route

The Bible

THE GREATEST STORY EVER READ

Like lots of action? Want to quickly get the gist of the great story of God? Here's a reading plan that will keep even a Bible novice turning the pages.

- **Genesis:** Learn about the beginning of humanity, sin, and God's plan to rescue the world.

- **Exodus 1–20:** Read about how God brings his chosen people out of bondage.

- **Numbers 10–25:** Read the story of the Israelites' fear and unbelief—and the tragic consequences.

- **Joshua:** Join Moses' protégé as he finally leads the people into the Promised Land.

- **Judges:** Watch the Israelites repeatedly fall away from God, suffer at the hands of their enemies, turn back to God, and experience deliverance via God-sent leaders.

- **1 and 2 Samuel:** See the rise and fall of King Saul and the rise of David during the lifetime of the prophet Samuel.

- **1 and 2 Kings:** Read about Solomon (David's son), the split of the nation of Israel, and the tragic demise of the two kingdoms, leading to the Assyrian conquest and Babylonian captivity.

- **Luke 1–2, Matthew 1–2, and the Gospel of Mark:** You can read all the four Gospels later, but these readings will give you a good snapshot of Christ's life.

- **Acts:** See the early church come to life and spread the gospel beginning in Jerusalem and, via Paul and others, throughout the Gentile (non-Jewish) world.

- **Revelation:** Though it's technically *prophecy* and not *history*, John's epic end-times vision peeks into the future and Jesus' ultimate triumph over evil.

Rose Publishing, Inc.   May be reproduced for classroom use only, not for sale.

65

The Basic Story of the Bible

God Creates.
Dates unknown
Genesis 1–2

God creates the world and puts Adam and Eve in the Garden of Eden.

Humanity sins.
Dates unknown
Genesis 3

Adam and Eve eat forbidden fruit and plunge the world into sin.

The world floods.
Dates unknown
Genesis 6–9

The human race deteriorates into evil. Only Noah and his family survive the catastrophic judgment of a colossal flood.

God saves.
1446 BC
Exodus–Leviticus

Moses leads the enslaved Israelites out of Egypt and to Mount Sinai where they receive the Ten Commandments and other laws for their charter as God's people.

Israel wanders.
1446–1406 BC
Numbers–Deuteronomy

Because of disbelief and disobedience, the Israelites wander in the desert south of Canaan for 40 years.

God blesses.
1406–1350 BC
Joshua

Joshua leads the Israelites in conquering and settling Canaan.

Israel defeated.
722 BC
2 Kings 17

When the prophets' warnings go unheeded, the Assyrian Empire conquers the northern kingdom of Israel. People flee, die, or are forced to relocate.

Judah exiled.
586 BC
2 Kings 18–25
2 Chronicles 36

God sends more prophets to warn his people. When their words are ignored, the Babylonian Empire conquers the southern kingdom of Judah.

Jews return.
538–430 BC
Ezra–Esther

Zerubbabel, then Ezra, and finally Nehemiah help relocate many of the Jews from Babylon. They rebuild the temple and the walls of Jerusalem.

(All dates are approximate.)

Nations rise.
Dates unknown
Genesis 10–11

God scatters the growing human race by causing them to speak different languages at the tower of Babel.

God chooses.
2100 BC
Genesis 12–36

God selects Abraham to be the father of many nations and promises worldwide blessing will come through his descendants.

God sustains.
1876 BC
Genesis 37–50

During a long famine, Abraham's grandson Jacob (a.k.a. Israel) and his family go to Egypt, where their descendants remain for about 400 years.

Judges deliver.
1350–1051 BC
Judges–Ruth

A series of judges functioning more like military leaders rescue and guide the nation.

Kings rule.
1051–931 BC
1 and 2 Samuel–1 Kings 11
1 Chronicles–2 Chronicles 9

Israelites clamor for a king. They get King Saul, then David, and then David's son Solomon.

Kingdom breaks up.
931–722 BC
1 Kings 12–2 Kings 17
2 Chronicles 10–35

Disagreement splits the kingdom: Israel in the north and Judah in the south. God's people drift into idolatry while prophets warn them of judgment.

Israel awaits the Messiah.
430–4 BC

During the time between the Old and New Testaments, Israel languishes under mostly foreign rule.

Messiah arrives.
4 BC–AD 30
Matthew–John

Jesus, the long-awaited Messiah, is born in Bethlehem. After spending about thirty years in relative obscurity, Jesus chooses and trains twelve disciples. He teaches, performs miracles, heals people, and shows people God's love. Jesus sacrificially dies on the cross and then rises from the dead three days later to provide a way to God the Father, by grace and through faith. Jesus then ascends to heaven.

The gospel spreads.
AD 30–96
Acts

Jesus' disciples, led primarily by Peter and Paul, spread the good news (the gospel) about Jesus, including the claim that he is coming again to bring history to a close and to complete the restoration of all things. The New Testament Scriptures are written, ending with the book of Revelation near the close of the first century.

Here's a chronological listing of the books, as grouped by era and theme.

Era	Theme	Books
THE BEGINNING Unknown–1805 BC	The introduction of God and humankind	Genesis, Job
THE LAW 1446–1406 BC	The Law given to the Hebrews as they wander in the desert	Exodus, Leviticus, Numbers, Deuteronomy
EARLY HEBREW HISTORY 1406–1051 BC	The Promised Land conquered and the people ruled by judges	Joshua, Judges, Ruth
LATER HEBREW HISTORY AND EARLY PROPHETS 1051–586 BC	The nation headed by kings; the spiritual struggles and eventual exile of the people	1 and 2 Samuel, 1 and 2 Kings, 1 and 2 Chronicles, Psalms, Proverbs, Ecclesiastes, Song of Songs, Isaiah, Jeremiah, Lamentations, Hosea, Amos, Jonah, Micah, Nahum, Habakkuk, Zephaniah
LATER PROPHETS 586–430 BC	Exile and then return of some people to the Promised Land	Ezra, Nehemiah, Esther, Ezekiel, Daniel, Joel, Obadiah, Haggai, Zechariah, Malachi
JESUS 4 BC–AD 30	The gospel (good news) about Jesus	Matthew, Mark, Luke, John
THE EARLY CHURCH AD 30–96	The church's numerical, geographical, and spiritual growth	Acts, Romans, 1 and 2 Corinthians, Galatians, Ephesians, Philippians, Colossians, 1 and 2 Thessalonians, 1 and 2 Timothy, Titus, Philemon, Hebrews, James, 1 and 2 Peter, 1, 2, and 3 John, Jude, Revelation

(Dates are approximate.)

Once we see how the Bible is organized, we get a clearer understanding of the essential story of the Bible. And when we realize the story is still unfolding, we get a new sense of purpose. We are somewhere between the final events detailed in Acts and the future events described in the book of Revelation. This means we are more than readers; we are characters in the great drama of God!

STORY NOTES

- Abraham and Job might have lived around the same time.

- From Exodus 19 to the book of Leviticus, the people of Israel are camped at Mount Sinai, receiving God's law and his plans for building the tabernacle—a kind of "traveling worship center."

- In Deuteronomy, Israel is gathered at Moab, just across the Jordan River from Canaan (the Promised Land). The only "action" in Deuteronomy is Moses reminding the younger generation of God's law and the covenant their parents made with God at Sinai.

- First and 2 Chronicles retell many of the stories from 1 and 2 Samuel and 1 and 2 Kings. Think of Chronicles as a "priestly editorial" mostly about King David and the southern kingdom of Judah.

- Ezekiel and Daniel prophesied during the time when God's people were taken into exile.

- The last three prophets—Haggai, Zechariah, and Malachi—come on the scene after the exile when the Jews return to their homeland.

- There's about a 400-year gap between where the Old Testament leaves off and the New Testament picks up.

- The New Testament begins with four biographies of Jesus, each named after the men who wrote them: Matthew, Mark, Luke, and John. These are called the Gospels, which means "good news."

- The fifth history book of the New Testament is Acts, which tells the story of the first Christians. Written by Luke, it picks up where his Gospel ends.

- Most of the letters (called epistles) of the New Testament were written during the period described in the book of Acts or shortly after.

Next, let's broaden our understanding by setting Bible history in context with other world events occurring at the same time, using the following time line.

Bible Events and World Events Side by Side

GENESIS, JOB

2100 BC	2000 BC	1900 BC	1800 BC

Dates for events before Abraham are unknown.

Abraham c. 2166–1991

Job (dates unknown)

Isaac c. 2066–1886

Jacob c. 2005–1859

Joseph c. 1914–1805

• Jacob and family leave to Egypt c. 1876

« God creates the world and Adam and Eve

« Noah's ark built, the flood

« Tower of Babel built

BIBLE EVENTS

WORLD EVENTS

11th and 12th dynasties, Egypt c. 2050–1800

« Earliest forms of writing (cuneiform), Mesopotamia c. 3200

• Ziggurats built, Ur c. 2100

Hammurabi reigns, Babylon c. 1792–1750

« Stonehenge erected, England c. 3000

Reconstruction of the Ziggurat at Ur, near Nasiriyah, Iraq

« Old kingdom pyramids built, Egypt c. 2700–2200

Egyptian hieroglyphics

2100 BC	2000 BC	1900 BC	1800 BC

EXODUS, LEVITICUS, NUMBERS, DEUTERONOMY			JOSHUA, JUDGES, RUTH	
1700 BC	1600 BC	1500 BC	1400 BC	1300 BC

Hebrews (Israelites) in Egypt c. 1876–1446

Era of Judges »

Moses c. 1526–1406

Ten Commandments

• First Passover,
the exodus c. 1446

• Ten Commandments;
the tabernacle c. 1446

Israelites wander in desert
c. 1446–1406

• Joshua leads the Israelites
into Canaan c. 1406

• Rahab helps save the spies
c. 1406

Some scholars date the exodus at 1290 BC; the era of the Judges would then begin at around 1130 BC.

• Shang dynasty begins,
China c. 1600

• Hittites sack Babylon
1595

King Tut, Egypt c. 1333–1323

Ramses I, Egypt 1318–1317

Dragon Gong, Shang
dynasty, 12th century BC

• 18th dynasty begins,
Egypt 1570

Death Mask of King Tut

| 1700 BC | 1600 BC | 1500 BC | 1400 BC | 1300 BC |

Bible Events and World Events Side by Side (cont.)

JOSHUA, JUDGES, RUTH	1 SAMUEL THROUGH 2 CHRONICLES

1300 BC   1200 BC   1100 BC   1000 BC   900 BC

Nation divides into •
Israel (northern kingdom) and
Judah (southern kingdom) 931

» Era of Judges (Deborah, Gideon, Samson, and others) c. 1350–1051

Ruth (dates unknown)

Eli, priest in Shiloh c. 1100–1060

Samuel, judge and prophet in Israel c. 1060–1020

King Saul, Israel's first king c. 1051–1011

King David c. 1011–971

Prophet Nathan c. 990–957

King Solomon
c. 971–931

•First temple in
Jerusalem built 960

Elijah c. 870–845

Kings are listed by dates of reign.

King David

BIBLE EVENTS

WORLD EVENTS

Ramses II, Egypt 1304–1237

•Mayan dynasties founded,
Central America c. 1000

Pharaoh Merneptah; his victory
stele is Israel's first recorded
mention in non-biblical history;
Egypt 1237–1227

•Iron Age begins;
Hittite Empire collapses
c. 1200

Hiram, king of Tyre
c. 978–944

•Trojan War begins,
Asia Minor (modern
day Turkey) c. 1190

Gran Jaguar, Mayan
temple, Guatemala

© William Cushman/Shutterstock.com

•Egypt's power begins
to decline c. 1164

Pharaoh Shishak
(Shoshenq) I,
Egypt 945–924

•Zhou (Chou) Dynasty begins,
China c. 1150

1300 BC   1200 BC   1100 BC   1000 BC   900 BC

ISAIAH THROUGH ZEPHANIAH, PSALMS THROUGH SONG OF SONGS   **EZRA, NEHEMIAH, ESTHER, HAGGAI, ZECHARIAH, MALACHI**

800 BC   700 BC   600 BC   500 BC   400 BC

Northern Kingdom of Israel

Southern Kingdom of Judah

Malachi c. 400s (dates unknown)

Joel (dates unknown)

Elisha c. 845–800

• Obadiah c. 586

Jonah c. 783–753

• Judah falls to Babylon; temple and Jerusalem destroyed; people carried into exile 586

Amos c. 760–753

• Cyrus the Great of Persia allows Jews to return to Judah 538

Isaiah c. 760–673

• Temple rebuilding in Jerusalem begins 536

Hosea c. 752–722

• Haggai c. 520

Micah c. 738–698

Zechariah c. 520–518

• Israel (northern kingdom) falls to Assyria 722

• Zerubbabel and Joshua the high priest lead the people to finish rebuilding the temple 516

Nahum c. 663–612

Zephaniah c. 641–628

• Queen Esther in Persia c. 478

Jeremiah c. 626–582

• Ezra goes to Judah 457

Ezekiel c. 620–570

Nehemiah governs Judah 444–432

Habakkuk c. 609–598

Nehemiah returns to Babylon c. 432–430

Daniel c. 605–535

Jeremiah

Prophets are listed by dates they prophesied.

Gautama Buddha, India c. 563–483

Greek poet Homer c. 800–701

• Aesop's Fables c. 560

Cyrus the Great, Persia 559–530

• First recorded Olympic games, Greece 776

Philosopher Confucius, China 551–479

• Founding of Rome 753

Confucius

• Babylon falls to Persia 539

• Roman Republic established 509

Athenian leader Pericles, Greece c. 500–429

Assyria rules Egypt 671–652

King Xerxes I (Ahasuerus), Persia 485–465

Babylonian mosaic

• Nineveh, capital of Assyria, falls to Babylonians and Medes 612

King Artaxerxes, Persia 464–424

800 BC   700 BC   600 BC   500 BC   400 BC

Bible Events and World Events Side by Side (cont.)

BETWEEN THE OLD AND NEW TESTAMENTS	THE GOSPELS: MATTHEW, MARK, LUKE, JOHN

| 400 BC | 300 BC | 200 BC | 100 BC | AD 1 | AD 10 | AD 20 | AD 30 |

None of the 66 books of the Bible cover this time period.

Jesus baptized by John the Baptist in •
the Jordan River c. 26

Birth of John the Baptist •
(parents: Zechariah and Elizabeth) c. 5 BC

Jesus' death on the cross and resurrection •
in Jerusalem c. 30

Birth of Jesus in Bethlehem •
(parents: Joseph and Mary) c. 4 BC

The risen Jesus appears to his twelve disciples and •
many others; ascends to heaven c. 30

Disciples receive the Holy•
Spirit during Pentecost c. 30

Stephen martyred in •
Jerusalem c. 32

Paul converted on the road•
to Damascus 37

BIBLE EVENTS

WORLD EVENTS

• Plato writes *The Republic* c. 370

Herod the Great, King of Judea 37–4

Alexander the Great establishes
the Alexandrian Empire 336–323

Caesar Augustus rules the Rome Empire 27 BC–AD 14

Herod Antipas rules Galilee 4 BC–AD 39

Septuagint •
(translation of Hebrew
Scriptures into Greek)
c. 255

Dead Sea Scrolls (copies of the Hebrew Scriptures) written c. 200 BC–AD 100

• Antiochus IV Epiphanes tries to
eradicate the Jewish religion 175

Caiaphas, high priest in Jerusalem 18–36

The Maccabean revolt and Hasmonean dynasty 166–63

Pontius Pilate governs
Judea 26–36

• Temple in Jerusalem rededicated (Hanukkah) c. 164

Spartacus leads slave revolt 73–71

• Rome rules Judea after Pompey
captures Jerusalem 63

Cleopatra VII rules Egypt 51–31

Hanukkah Menorah

Caesar Augustus

| 400 BC | 300 BC | 200 BC | 100 BC | AD 1 | AD 10 | AD 20 | AD 30 |

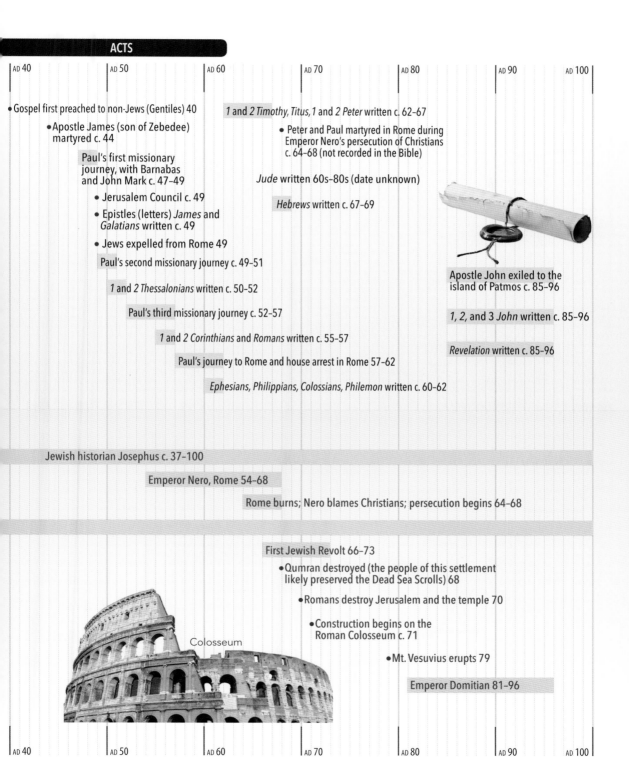

ACTS

AD 40 — AD 50 — AD 60 — AD 70 — AD 80 — AD 90 — AD 100

- Gospel first preached to non-Jews (Gentiles) 40
  - Apostle James (son of Zebedee) martyred c. 44
    - Paul's first missionary journey, with Barnabas and John Mark c. 47–49
      - Jerusalem Council c. 49
      - Epistles (letters) *James* and *Galatians* written c. 49
      - Jews expelled from Rome 49
      - Paul's second missionary journey c. 49–51
        - *1* and *2 Thessalonians* written c. 50–52
          - Paul's third missionary journey c. 52–57
            - *1* and *2 Corinthians* and *Romans* written c. 55–57
              - Paul's journey to Rome and house arrest in Rome 57–62
                - *Ephesians, Philippians, Colossians, Philemon* written c. 60–62

1 and *2 Timothy, Titus, 1* and *2 Peter* written c. 62–67
- Peter and Paul martyred in Rome during Emperor Nero's persecution of Christians c. 64–68 (not recorded in the Bible)

Jude written 60s–80s (date unknown)

Hebrews written c. 67–69

Apostle John exiled to the island of Patmos c. 85–96

1, 2, and *3 John* written c. 85–96

Revelation written c. 85–96

Jewish historian Josephus c. 37–100

Emperor Nero, Rome 54–68

Rome burns; Nero blames Christians; persecution begins 64–68

First Jewish Revolt 66–73
- Qumran destroyed (the people of this settlement likely preserved the Dead Sea Scrolls) 68
  - Romans destroy Jerusalem and the temple 70
  - Construction begins on the Roman Colosseum c. 71
    - Mt. Vesuvius erupts 79

Emperor Domitian 81–96

Colosseum

AD 40 — AD 50 — AD 60 — AD 70 — AD 80 — AD 90 — AD 100

Kings of Israel and Judah

THE KINGS OF ISRAEL (NORTHERN KINGDOM)

900 BC   800 BC   700 BC   600 BC   500 BC

Jeroboam I 931–910

Nadab 910–909

Baasha 909–886

Elah 886–885

Zimri 885

Tibni 885–880

Omri 885–874

Ahab 874–853

Ahaziah 853–852

Joram (Jehoram) 852–841

Jehu 841–814

Jehoahaz 814–798

Jehoash 798–792

Jeroboam II 793–753

Zechariah 753

Shallum 752

Menahem 752–742

Pekah 752–732

Pekahiah 742–740

Hoshea 732–722

• Northern kingdom falls to the Assyrian Empire 722

THE KINGS OF JUDAH (SOUTHERN KINGDOM)

900 BC   800 BC   700 BC   600 BC   500 BC

Rehoboam I 931–913

Abijah 913–911

Asa 911–870

Jehoshaphat 873–848

Jehoram (Joram) 853–841

Ahaziah 841

Queen Athaliah 841–835

Joash 835–796

Amaziah 796–767

Uzziah (Azariah) 792–740

Jotham 750–735

Ahaz (Jehoahaz) 735–716

Hezekiah 716–687

Manasseh 697–643

Amon 643–641

Josiah 641–609

Jehoahaz (Shallum) 609

Jehoiakim (Eliakim) 609–598

Jehoiachin (Jeconiah) 598–597

Zedekiah (Mattaniah) 597–586

• Southern kingdom falls to the Babylonian Empire 586

Chapter 4

MEETING THE CHARACTERS:
A WHO'S WHO OF BIBLE PEOPLE

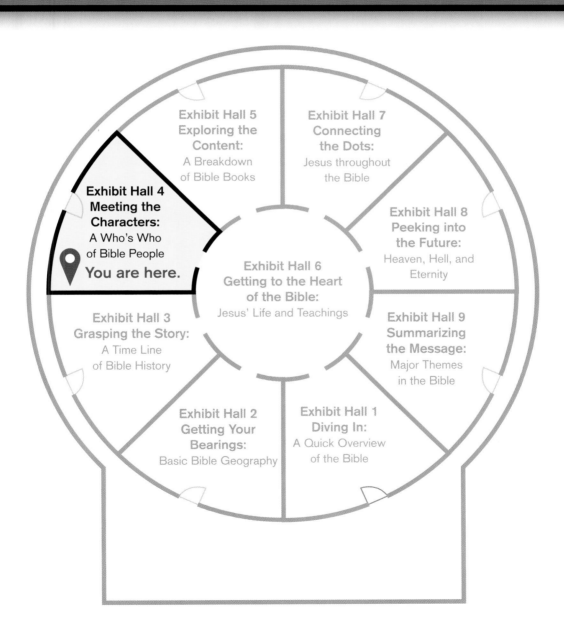

Exhibit Hall 5
Exploring the Content:
A Breakdown of Bible Books

Exhibit Hall 7
Connecting the Dots:
Jesus throughout the Bible

**Exhibit Hall 4
Meeting the Characters:**
A Who's Who of Bible People
You are here.

Exhibit Hall 8
Peeking into the Future:
Heaven, Hell, and Eternity

Exhibit Hall 6
Getting to the Heart of the Bible:
Jesus' Life and Teachings

Exhibit Hall 3
Grasping the Story:
A Time Line of Bible History

Exhibit Hall 9
Summarizing the Message:
Major Themes in the Bible

Exhibit Hall 2
Getting Your Bearings:
Basic Bible Geography

Exhibit Hall 1
Diving In:
A Quick Overview of the Bible

Exhibit Hall 4

With more than 3,000 named characters (and many others unnamed), the Bible routinely causes readers to wrinkle their brows and pose questions like . . .

"Who's this guy again?"

"What's her connection to him?"

"*Another* Mary?"

We feel your pain! So this is the place in your *Self-Guided Tour of the Bible* where you'll find fast facts and brief bios of about one hundred of the main characters in Scripture.

Let's start with the thirty biggest biblical personalities. For the sake of easy reference, we'll list them in alphabetical order. (Note: Many dates are estimates only; c. = approximate date. Dates reflect the time span that the person appears in Bible history, not necessarily dates of birth and death which are unknown in many cases.)

ABRAHAM (ABRAM) – "God's friend"

When & where: c. 2166–1991 BC in Mesopotamia (Ur), Canaan, and Egypt

Read about him in: Genesis 11:27–25:11; Matthew 1:1–2; Acts 7:2–8; Hebrews 11:8–12

Significance: The father of the Hebrew people and considered a paragon of faith

Key facts & events:

- Husband to Sarah (Sarai) and uncle of Lot
- Obeyed God's late-in-life calling to leave Mesopotamia and go to Canaan
- Father of Ishmael (via his wife's servant Hagar) and then (with Sarah) Isaac—the child promised by God
- Despite doubting God on multiple occasions, was called "God's friend" (James 2:23)
- Died at 175 years of age and was buried in Canaan next to his wife, Sarah

ADAM – The first man

When & where: Dates unknown; the Garden of Eden and elsewhere in Mesopotamia

Read about him in: Genesis 1:26–5:5; Luke 3:38; Romans 5:14; 1 Corinthians 15:22, 45

Exhibit Hall 4

Significance: The first person ever created by God and the father of the human race

Key facts & events:

- Eve's husband and the father of Cain, Abel, Seth, and other unnamed children
- Ate the forbidden fruit given to him by Eve from the tree of the knowledge of good and evil
- With Eve, banished from the Garden of Eden for his disobedience to God
- Died at the age of 930

DANIEL – The man in the lions' den

When & where: c. 605–535 BC in Judah and Babylon

Read about him in: Ezekiel 14:14, 20; 28:3; the book of Daniel; Matthew 24:15–16; Mark 13:14

Significance: A high-ranking government official in Babylon and visionary Jewish prophet

Key facts & events:

- A member of Judah's elite upper class taken captive, transported to Babylon, and pressed into civil service
- Miraculously saved by God when thrown into a den of hungry lions for refusing to stop praying to God
- A gifted interpreter of dreams and visions
- A man of self-control (Daniel 1:8), prayer (2:1–18), bold courage (5:22–23), and sterling character (6:4–23)

DAVID – The giant slayer

When & where: c. 1040–971 BC in Israel (especially Bethlehem, Hebron, and Jerusalem)

Read about him in: 1 Samuel 16–30; the book of 2 Samuel; 1 Chronicles 17; Matthew 1:6; John 7:42; Acts 2:29–31; 13:22, 36; Hebrews 11:32

Significance: Israel's greatest king, Solomon's father, a shepherd, a skilled musician, and the author of about half the psalms

Key facts & events:

- Became a living legend when he killed the giant Goliath with his slingshot

- On the run from the paranoid, murderous King Saul for years before becoming Israel's king
- Committed adultery with Bathsheba and arranged for her husband, Uriah, to be killed in battle; when confronted, he repented of this sin.
- Known as a man after God's own heart (1 Samuel 13:14)

ELIJAH – The man who never died

When & where: c. 870–845 BC in Israel

Read about him in: 1 Kings 17–19; 21; 2 Kings 1–2; Malachi 4:5; Matthew 11:14; 16:14; 17:1–11; Mark 9:2–13; Luke 1:17; 9:7–9, 19, 28–36

Significance: A fearless prophet of the Lord who thundered against rampant idolatry in Israel

Key facts & events:

- A contemporary (and nemesis) of King Ahab (and Queen Jezebel) of Israel
- Performed dazzling miracles like raising a boy from the dead
- Defeated the false prophets of Baal and Asherah on Mount Carmel
- "Beamed up" to heaven in a whirlwind without dying
- Appeared with Moses at Christ's transfiguration

ESTHER – The queen who saved her people

When & where: c. 478 BC in Susa, the capital of Persia

Read about her in: The book that bears her name

Significance: The Jewish queen of Persia who used her beauty and position to save her people from genocide

Key facts & events:

- A younger relative of Mordecai (who became Esther's guardian)
- Chosen by King Xerxes to be the new queen
- Working with Mordecai, Esther boldly pled for the lives of her people, and won Xerxes' favor (shown by his executing Haman, the enemy of the Jews)

EVE – The first woman

When & where: Dates unknown; the Garden of Eden and elsewhere in Mesopotamia

Read about her in: Genesis 2:18–4:2; 2 Corinthians 11:3; 1 Timothy 2:13

Significance: Adam's wife and the world's first woman

Key facts & events:

- Wife to Adam and the mother of Cain, Abel, Seth, and other unnamed children
- Created in the image of God and with Adam appointed a co-ruler of creation
- Listened to the temptation of Satan (the serpent) and ate the forbidden fruit from the tree of the knowledge of good and evil
- With Adam, banished from the Garden of Eden for disobedience to God

EZEKIEL – A man of many strange visions

When & where: c. 597–571 BC in Judah and Babylon

Read about him in: The book that bears his name

Significance: A priest-turned-prophet who ministered to Jewish exiles during the Babylonian captivity

Key facts & events:

- Was the recipient of strange and mysterious visions by God
- Had a vision of a valley of dry bones that came to life—a message of hope for the exiled Jews
- According to tradition, he was killed by his countrymen for denouncing their idolatry

EZRA – A godly priest and scribe

When & where: c. 457–444 BC in Babylon and Jerusalem

Read about him in: Ezra 7:1–10:16; Nehemiah 8:1–12:36

Significance: A learned Jewish scribe and priest who led the Jews back to Jerusalem after the exile

Key facts & events:

- His name means "help."
- A committed student and teacher of God's Word; may have written Ezra and 1 and 2 Chronicles
- Worked with Nehemiah in trying to spark a spiritual awakening among the Jews returning from Babylonian captivity

ISAAC – The promised son

When & where: c. 2066–1886 BC in Canaan

Read about him in: Genesis 17:15–28:9; 35:27–29; Romans 9:7–10; Hebrews 11:20

Significance: The promised son of Abraham and Sarah, and the father of Jacob and Esau

Key facts & events:

- Born when his father was 100 and his mother 90
- His name means "laughter."
- Married to Rebekah, with whom he had fraternal twin sons, Esau and Jacob

ISAIAH – The messianic prophet

When & where: c. 760–673 BC in Judah and Jerusalem

Read about him in: 2 Kings 19–20; 2 Chronicles 26:22; 32:20, 32; the book that bears his name

Significance: The prophet who both warned of judgment and predicted future hope for God's people

Key facts & events:

- Married to a prophetess and had two sons
- Prophesied in great detail about the coming Messiah—his virgin birth, mission, death, and future reign
- Quoted extensively by the New Testament writers

JACOB (ISRAEL) – The man who wrestled with God

When & where: c. 2005–1859 BC in Israel and the surrounding region

Read about him in: Genesis 25–50

Significance: The grandson of Abraham; father of twelve sons whose descendants became Israel's twelve tribes

Key facts & events:

- Son of Isaac and Rebekah, younger twin brother of Esau, husband of Rachel and Leah

- Favorite son of his mother who helped him deceive his blind father into giving him the blessing normally given to the oldest son

- Despite his shrewd character and trickery, he was the recipient of much grace from God.

- After wrestling with the angel of the Lord, God changed his name to Israel, which means "struggle."

JEREMIAH – The weeping prophet

When & where: c. 626–582 BC in Judah

Read about him in: 2 Chronicles 35:25; 36:11–21; Ezra 1:1; the books of Jeremiah and Lamentations; Daniel 9:2

Significance: Often called "the weeping prophet"; ministered during the destruction of Judah (Jeremiah 9:1)

Key facts & events:

- Persecuted for his persistent efforts to communicate God's truth: accused of treason, assaulted, arrested, and imprisoned

- Authored the book that bears his name and the book of Lamentations

Exhibit Hall 4

JOB – The man who lost it all

When & Where: Dates unknown (possibly c. 2100 BC) in the land of Uz (location unknown)

Read about him in: the book that bears his name; also Ezekiel 14:14, 20 and James 5:11

Significance: Tormented by Satan (with God's permission) in order to demonstrate that God is sovereign, holy, good, and worthy of worship, even during times of suffering

Key facts & events:

- A man of impeccable character and great wealth who experienced devastating loss of his children, possessions, and health (Job 1–3)
- Counseled (not always wisely) by his friends (Job 4–37)
- Experienced a powerful encounter with God and restoration after his trials (Job 38–42)

JOHN THE APOSTLE – The beloved disciple

When & where: c. AD 26–96 in Israel and Asia Minor, the Island of Patmos

Read about him in: Matthew, Mark, Luke, and the books he wrote: John, 1, 2, and 3 John; and Revelation

Significance: Fisherman-turned-follower of Jesus and part of Jesus' inner circle: Peter, James, and John

Key facts & events:

- The son of Zebedee and brother to James
- Was one of the "sons of thunder," a nickname given by Jesus to him and his brother for their feisty personalities (Mark 3:17)
- Referred to himself as "the disciple whom Jesus loved" (John 13:23; 20:2; 21:7, 20)
- Was asked by Jesus on the cross to care for Jesus' mother, Mary (John 19:26–27)

JOHN THE BAPTIST – The harbinger of Jesus

When & where: c. 5 BC–AD 28 in Israel and the wilderness of Judea

Read about him in: Matthew 3; Mark 1:1–8; 9:11–13; Luke 1:5–15, 57–63; 3:1–20; 7:18–35; 9:7–9; 11:1; 16:16; 20:4–6; Acts 1:5; 10:37; 11:16; 13:24–25; 18:25; 19:3–4

Significance: The miracle child of elderly parents; introduced Jesus to the world and baptized him

Key facts & events:

- Son of Elizabeth and Zechariah and a relative of Jesus through Mary
- Wore camel's hair clothing and lived on a diet of locusts and wild honey
- Preached fiery sermons calling people to repentance and baptized those who repented
- Beheaded by Herod Antipas for boldly confronting the king's adultery

JOSEPH – A slave-turned-Egyptian-ruler

When & where: c. 1914–1805 BC in Canaan and Egypt

Read about him in: Genesis 30:22–24; 37; 39–50; Exodus 1:5–7; Psalm 105:16–24; Acts 7:9–14; Hebrews 11:22

Significance: Favorite son of Jacob; used by God to save many lives during a time of famine

Key facts & events:

- Given a coat of many colors by his father Jacob
- Had an ability to interpret dreams
- Sold into slavery by his jealous brothers and ended up in Egypt
- Sent to prison for a crime he did not commit, but later rose to become second only to Pharaoh in power
- Came face to face with his terrified brothers when they had traveled to Egypt in search of food because of a severe famine in Canaan
- Forgave his brothers and insisted that God had been the one who sent him to Egypt for a much greater purpose

JOSHUA – A courageous leader and warrior

When & where: c. 1406 BC in Egypt, the wilderness south of Canaan, and Canaan itself

Read about him in: Exodus 17:8–15; Numbers 11:28; 26:65; 27:12–23; 32; 34; Deuteronomy 31; the book that bears his name; Judges 1–2; 1 Kings 16:34; Acts 7:45; Hebrews 4:8

Significance: The protégé and successor to Moses who led the twelve tribes in conquering and settling the Promised Land

Key facts & events:

- An experienced warrior and one of the twelve men chosen to spy out the Promised Land
- His name means "the Lord is salvation"—the Hebrew version of "Jesus."

MARY – Jesus' mother

When & where: c. 4 BC–AD 30 in Israel (Nazareth, Bethlehem, and Jerusalem) and a short time in Egypt

Read about her in: Isaiah 7:14; Matthew 1–2; 13:55; Mark 6:3; Luke 1:26–56; 2; John 19:25–27; Acts 1:14

Significance: Chosen by God to give birth to the Savior of the world

Key facts & events:

- Was told by an angel—before her marriage to Joseph and while still a virgin—that she would miraculously bear a son, Jesus, through the power of the Holy Spirit
- Was submissive to the Lord and reflected upon the work of God in her life (Luke 1:38; 2:19)
- Was at the cross when Jesus died; after Jesus' death, she was taken into the apostle John's home to be cared for as his own mother

MATTHEW (LEVI) – The tax-collecting disciple

When & where: c. AD 26–60s in Israel

Read about him in: Matthew 9–10; Mark 2; Luke 5–6; Acts 1:13

Significance: A former tax collector called by Jesus to become an apostle

Key facts & events:

- Upon deciding to follow Jesus, threw a big party and invited Jesus' entourage and all his old tax collector friends
- Wrote the Gospel that bears his name

MOSES – The man who defied Pharaoh

When & where: c. 1526–1406 BC in Egypt, Sinai, and the wilderness south and east of Canaan

Read about him in: Exodus; Deuteronomy; Psalm 105:26–41; Matthew 17:3; Acts 7:20–44; Hebrews 3:1–5; 11:23–29

Significance: Israel's deliverer and lawgiver who led God's people out of Egypt to the border of the Promised Land and authored the first five books of the Old Testament

Key facts & events:

- From the tribe of Levi; brother to Aaron and Miriam
- As an infant, placed by his mother in a basket in the Nile River, so he could be found by Pharaoh's compassionate daughter instead of killed due to Pharaoh's murderous decree
- Forced to flee Egypt after killing an abusive Egyptian taskmaster
- Called by God from a burning bush and commissioned to return to Egypt to lead God's people out of slavery
- Confronted the hard-hearted Pharaoh who—after ten horrible plagues upon Egypt—finally relented and let God's people leave
- Led the people through the miraculous parting of the Red Sea and into Sinai where God gave him the Ten Commandments, the laws, and instructions for building the tabernacle (a sacred tent where God met with his people in the wilderness)
- Forbidden by God to enter the Promised Land because of an angry outburst
- Died on Mount Nebo in Moab and was buried by God

NEHEMIAH – The wall builder

When & where: c. 444–430 BC in Persia and Jerusalem

Read about him in: Ezra 2:2 and the book that bears his name

Significance: Led the final of three return trips from Persia to Jerusalem after the Babylonian exile and oversaw the rebuilding of the walls of Jerusalem

Key facts & events:

- A prominent Jew who worked for King Artaxerxes of Persia
- Was concerned enough about his homeland to return to Jerusalem and lead a ragtag group in a massive wall-building project that took only fifty-two days to complete

NOAH – The man who built a huge boat

When & where: Dates unknown; Mesopotamia

Read about him in: Genesis 5:28–9:29 Hebrews 11:7; 1 Peter 3:20; 2 Peter 2:5

Significance: Constructed a massive boat (ark) at God's command in which he survived the great flood along with his family and many animals

Key facts & events:

- Father of three sons: Shem, Ham, and Japheth
- Received God's favor (grace) and was called "a righteous man" who "walked faithfully with God" (Genesis 6:8–9)
- Died at the age of 950

PAUL (SAUL) – A Pharisee-turned-Christian-missionary

When & where: c. AD 32–68 in Israel and "on the road" all over the Roman Empire

Read about him in: Acts 7–28, 2 Peter 3:15–16, and Paul's letters: Romans, 1 and 2 Corinthians, Galatians, Ephesians, Philippians, Colossians, 1 and 2 Thessalonians, 1 and 2 Timothy, Titus, and Philemon

Significance: Preeminent missionary, church planter, author, and theologian of the early church

Key facts & events:

- A native of Tarsus (in Cilicia), Roman citizen, and Pharisee who initially persecuted Christians

- Had a dramatic, life-changing encounter with the risen Christ on the road to Damascus

- Made three extensive missionary journeys in the Mediterranean region that are recorded in Acts

- Endured great physical hardship in his ministry for Christ (2 Corinthians 6; 11)

- Wrote thirteen of the twenty-seven books of the New Testament

- Tradition says he was beheaded outside Rome on the Appian Way.

PETER – The "rock"

When & where: c. AD 26–68 in and around Israel

Read about him in: The books of Matthew, Mark, Luke, and John; Acts 1–12; 15:7–11; and his two epistles: 1 and 2 Peter

Significance: A bold, brash fisherman who became Christ's most outspoken disciple and leader of the early church

Key facts & events:

- Birth name Simon; nickname Peter, given to him by Christ, from the Greek word *petros*, which means "rock"

- Fiercely loyal and prone to speak first and think later

- Only man (other than Jesus) to walk on water (Matthew 14:28–32)

- Denied knowing Jesus, but his relationship with Jesus was later restored; became the leader of the early church (John 18:15–27; 21:15–25)

- Instrumental in opening the door of the gospel to non-Jews (Acts 10)

RUTH – A foreigner redeemed

When & where: Dates unknown (Sometime during the era of judges: c. 1350–1051 BC) in Moab and Bethlehem

Read about her in: The book that bears her name and in Jesus' genealogy in Matthew 1:5

Significance: The Moabite daughter-in-law of Naomi; married Boaz and became King David's great-grandmother

Key facts & events:

- Returned to Israel with Naomi after their husbands died in Moab
- Famous for refusing to separate from her mother-in-law
- Regarded as a paragon of faithfulness during the dark time of the judges (when evil was rampant in Israel)

SAMUEL – The man who anointed kings

When & where: c. 1060–1020 BC in Israel

Read about him in: 1 Samuel 1–3; 7–13; 15–16; 19; 25:1; 28; 2 Chronicles 35:18; Psalm 99:6; Acts 3:24; 13:20

Significance: Israel's final judge and first great prophet (since Moses); anointed Israel's first two kings: Saul and David

Key facts & events:

- Given back to God by his godly mother, Hannah; raised at the tabernacle by the high priest Eli
- A Nazirite (i.e., one who drinks no alcohol and gets no haircuts) from birth

---

SARAH (SARAI) – Mother of the promised son

When & where: c. 2156–2029 BC in Mesopotamia and Canaan

Read about her in: Genesis 11–23; Romans 4:19; 9:9; Hebrews 11:11; 1 Peter 3:6

Significance: Abraham's wife and Isaac's mother

Key facts & events:

- In a crisis of faith, asked Abraham to give her a child via her servant Hagar
- Bore a son, Isaac, in her old age, just as God had promised her years before
- Despite lapses in faith, the first woman listed in the great "faith chapter" (Hebrews 11)

SAUL – Israel's first king

When & where: c. 1051–1011 BC in Israel

Read about him in: 1 Samuel 9–11; 13–24; 26–28; 31; Acts 13:21

Significance: Israel's first king, who turned away from God

Key facts & events:

- Extremely tall and handsome (1 Samuel 9:2)
- Father of Jonathan (David's dearest friend and ally) and Michal (David's first wife)
- Rejected as king for his disobedience to God, increasingly jealous of David, and then paranoid
- Repeatedly tried to kill David and ended up taking his own life rather than die at the hands of the Philistines he was battling

SOLOMON – The (mostly) wise king

When & where: c. 971–931 BC in Jerusalem

Read about him in: 2 Samuel 12:24; 1 Kings 1–11; 2 Kings 24:13; 1 Chronicles 22:5–17; 23:1; 28–29; Matthew 12:42

Significance: King David's son who ruled over Israel during its time of greatest glory; famous for his wisdom

Key facts & events:

- Son of David and Bathsheba
- Built Israel's first temple in Jerusalem
- Later in life, foolishly took 700 foreign wives (many of them political alliances) and 300 concubines, and turned to other gods
- Author of most of Proverbs and all of Ecclesiastes and the Song of Songs

The Biggest Character of All

GOD

Genesis opens with the words "in the beginning God" (Genesis 1:1). At the outset, the main character of the Bible makes his grand entrance. The Bible is *God's* story. It tells of *his* world and *his* plan to restore all that was lost when Adam and Eve sinned.

The Bible reveals that God is triune in his nature—literally a trinity in unity—one God existing eternally in three persons: Father, Son, and Holy Spirit.

"May the grace of the Lord Jesus Christ, and the love of God, and the fellowship of the Holy Spirit be with you all." —2 Corinthians 13:14

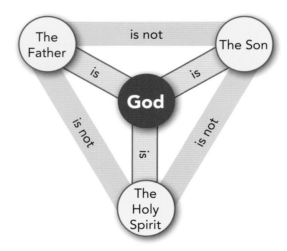

The Bible further describes God as . . .

1. The infinite Creator (Genesis 1–2)

2. The sovereign (authoritative, "in control") ruler and sustainer of life (Psalm 115:3; Isaiah 46:4)

3. Humankind's gracious helper and Savior (Psalm 54:4; Luke 1:47)

4. The just judge of the earth (Psalm 98:9)

In its 1,000+ pages, the Bible shows and tells us much, much more about God, its main character. But those four descriptions make a pretty good "quick list."

JESUS

Through stories that suggest, characters who foreshadow, rituals that symbolize, and prophecies that predict, the entire Old Testament hints at and points to the coming of Jesus.

He is the hero of God's story. Fully God and fully man—eternal yet born in time—Jesus lived a perfect life, willingly endured a gruesome death to pay the penalty of humankind's sins, and then was raised from the dead to give new life to all who believe. His story is told and his ministry is described in the Gospels, the first four books of the New Testament: Matthew, Mark, Luke, and John.

Before Jesus returned to heaven, he told his followers to go into the entire world with his good news of forgiveness and new, eternal life. And he assured them he will come to earth a second time to restore the universe to its original design. The book of Acts, along with the rest of the New Testament, documents their work and the beginnings of the worldwide Christian movement.

THE HOLY SPIRIT

Mentions of the "Spirit of God" or "Holy Spirit" (the third person of the holy Trinity) are found throughout the Bible. He was active in creation (Genesis 1:2). And he occasionally empowered Old Testament saints for mighty acts (Judges 14:6; 1 Samuel 16:13). But even when there's no overt mention of the Spirit, his invisible but real presence pervades the story of God from beginning to end.

It was not until the end of his ministry that Jesus began to talk more explicitly about the coming of the Spirit (John 14–16). Then, after Jesus left this world and the Holy Spirit was sent down to empower believers, the Spirit emerged as a central player throughout the book of Acts. In that one book, the Holy Spirit is mentioned almost sixty times!

It is the Spirit of God—the same Spirit who hovered over creation and who filled David and Jesus—who lives in and empowers modern-day believers. Is he living in *you*?

Spiritual Beings

SATAN

Who is the talking serpent who tempted Adam and Eve to evil in the Garden of Eden? A comprehensive study of the Old and New Testaments reveals a creature with various titles:

- *Satan*, Hebrew for "accuser" (Job 1:6–12)
- Lucifer (Isaiah 14:12 KJV)
- The devil (Matthew 4:1–11)
- The adversary (1 Peter 5:8 NASB)
- The father of lies (John 8:44)
- Beelzebul (Matthew 12:24)

This spirit opposes God—and everything and everyone that is near and dear to God's heart (John 10:10; 1 Peter 5:8). He is described as the ruler of a host of other fallen angels, which are demons (Matthew 25:41), and a powerful force in this world (2 Corinthians 4:4; Ephesians 6:12). The Bible assures us that Jesus—through his death and resurrection—came to defeat the devil and destroy his works (1 John 3:8).

ANGELS

Angels are among the Bible's great mysteries. These powerful, spiritual beings remain invisible, except for rare moments when they make dramatic entrances into the lives and events of biblical characters.

The Greek word for angel means "messenger," which describes their primary role throughout the pages of Scripture (Genesis 28:12; 2 Kings 1:15; Numbers 22:22; Matthew 28:2; Luke 1:28; Acts 5:19). In addition to serving as God's messengers and aides, angels surround God's throne and offer regular worship (Isaiah 6:1–2; Revelation 5:11). The Bible indicates that angels are obedient servants of God and coworkers in his plan (Psalm 103:20). Angels who succumbed to sin became demons (fallen angels) and placed their allegiance with Satan (2 Peter 2:4; Revelation 12:9).

Other Important Bible Characters

Aaron – The older brother of Moses and Israel's first high priest. c. 1529–1407 BC (Exodus–Numbers; Deuteronomy 10:6; 1 Chronicles 6:49–50; Psalms 99:6; 133:2; Micah 6:4; Hebrews 5:4; 9:4)

Abel – The second son of Adam and Eve, murdered by his brother Cain. Dates unknown (Genesis 4)

Abigail – A beautiful woman who married David after the death of her first husband, Nabal, a notorious fool. c. 1000 BC (1 Samuel 25; 27:3; 30:5)

Andrew – The fisherman-turned-disciple and brother of Peter. c. AD 26–60 (Matthew 4:18–19; 10:2; John 1:40–44; 6:8–9; 12:20–22)

Anna – A faithful, old Jewish prophetess who recognized and greeted the infant Jesus when he was presented at the temple. c. 4 BC (Luke 2:36–38)

Barnabas – A Levite from Cyprus who became one of Paul's ministry partners and an encouragement to all he met. c. AD 30–50 (Acts 4:36; 9:27; 11–15; Galatians 2; Colossians 4:10)

Bartholomew (a.k.a. Nathanael) – One of Jesus' twelve disciples, called by Jesus "an Israelite in whom there is no deceit" (John 1:47). c. AD 26–30 (Matthew 10:3; Mark 3:18; Luke 6:14; John 1:45–49; 21:2; Acts 1:13)

Bathsheba – The widow of Uriah, wife of King David, and mother of Solomon. c. 1000 BC (2 Samuel 11–12)

Boaz – The husband of Ruth, great-grandfather of David, and ancestor of Christ. Dates unknown; sometime during the era of judges: c. 1350–1050 BC (the book of Ruth; Matthew 1:5–6)

Cain – The first child born in the world, son of Adam and Eve, and murderer of Abel, his younger brother. Dates unknown (Genesis 4)

Caleb – Joshua's fellow spy and faithful sidekick who urged the reluctant Israelites to take the Promised Land against the cowardly counsel of the other ten spies. c. 1446 BC (Numbers 13–14; 26:65; 32:12; 34:19; Deuteronomy 1:36)

Cyrus – The Persian king who conquered the Babylonians and allowed the exiled Jews to return home and rebuild Jerusalem—as predicted by the prophet Isaiah some 150 years earlier (Isaiah 44:28). c. 538 BC (2 Chronicles 36:22–23)

Deborah – Prophetess and only female judge of Israel in the Bible; helped Barak defeat the Canaanites. Dates unknown; Sometime during the era of judges: c. 1350–1050 BC (Judges 4–5)

Eli – Israelite high priest who raised the prophet Samuel and died in shock upon hearing how the Philistines captured the ark of the covenant. c. 1100–1060 BC (1 Samuel 1–4)

Elisha – The prophet who succeeded Elijah and performed great miracles. c. 845–800 BC (2 Kings 2–5)

Elizabeth – Wife of the priest Zechariah; had a miracle pregnancy and gave birth to John the Baptist. c. 5 BC (Luke 1)

Enoch – One of two Old Testament people who went to heaven without dying (the other was Elijah). Dates unknown (Genesis 5:23–24; Hebrews 11:5)

Esau – Jacob's twin brother and the father of the Edomites. c. 2005–1859 BC (Genesis 25–33)

Gideon – The judge of Israel who defeated a vast enemy army with a mere 300 men. Dates unknown; sometime during the era of judges: c. 1350–1050 BC (Judges 6–8; Hebrews 11:32)

Hagar – The servant of Sarah and mother of Abraham's son Ishmael. c. 2090 BC (Genesis 16; 21; Galatians 4:24–25)

Hannah – The prophet Samuel's godly mother who presented him back to the Lord. c. 1100 BC (1 Samuel 1–2)

Herod Antipas – A son of Herod the Great. He had John the Baptist beheaded. He also sent Jesus back to Pontius Pilate to stand trial. c. 4 BC–AD 39 (Matthew 14:1–6; Luke 23:8–11; Acts 12)

Herod the Great – The king of Judea during the birth of Jesus; attempted to kill the child Jesus. c. 37–4 BC (Matthew 2)

Hezekiah – The son of the wicked King Ahaz and the thirteenth king of Judah who was the God-honoring leader who experienced God's deliverance from the invading Assyrian army. c. 716–687 BC (2 Kings 16:20–20:21; 2 Chronicles 28:27–32:33; Isaiah 36–39)

Hosea – Israelite prophet called by God to marry an adulterous woman to illustrate the nation's spiritual unfaithfulness. c. 752–722 BC (the book of Hosea)

Ishmael – Abraham's first son (with Sarah's servant Hagar). c. 2080–1943 BC (Genesis 17; 25; 28:9; 36:3)

Jezebel – The wicked queen and wife of King Ahab of Israel who violently opposed the prophet Elijah. c. 870 BC (1 Kings 16:31; 18–19, 21; 2 Kings 9:33–37)

Jonah – A reluctant prophet who delivered his message to Nineveh only after the Lord caused a great fish to swallow him. c. 783–753 BC (book of Jonah; Matthew 12:39–41; 16:4)

Jonathan – Son of King Saul and David's closest friend. c. 1020 BC (1 Samuel 13–14; 18–20)

Joseph, stepfather of Jesus – Husband of Mary and legal (though not biological) father of Jesus. c. 4 BC (Matthew 1–2; Luke 1–2)

Josiah – Judah's sixteenth king; a godly man who led the nation in a great revival. c. 641–609 BC (2 Kings 21:24–23:34)

Judas Iscariot – The disciple who betrayed Jesus for thirty pieces of silver and then committed suicide. AD 27–30 (Matthew 27; Mark 14:10–11; John 12:4; 13:2, 26)

Jude (a.k.a. Judas) – Half brother of Jesus and author of the epistle Jude. c. AD 60s–80s (Matthew 13:55; Mark 6:3; book of Jude)

Lazarus – Brother of Martha and Mary; resurrected by Jesus. c. AD 29 (John 11–12)

Leah – Sister of Rachel; Jacob's first wife, and the mother of six of his sons and daughter Dinah. c. 2005–1859 BC (Genesis 29–33)

Women in Jesus' Genealogy

Five women are mentioned in Jesus' genealogy in Matthew 1:1–17.

Tamar

Rahab

Ruth

Bathsheba

Mary (Jesus' mother)

Lot – Abraham's nephew who fled the city of Sodom when God brought judgment on the city. c. 2100 BC (Genesis 11:27–31; 12:4–5; 13–14; 19)

Luke – Gentile physician who traveled with the apostle Paul and wrote the Gospel of Luke and the book of Acts. c. AD 49–70s (Acts 16; 20–21; 27–28; Colossians 4:14; 2 Timothy 4:11; Philemon 24)

Mark (a.k.a. John Mark) – The cousin of Barnabas who failed in ministry on the first missionary journey but later became a great servant of Christ; wrote the Gospel that bears his name. c. AD 47–70s (Acts 13:13; 15:37–39; Colossians 4:10; 2 Timothy 4:11)

Martha – Sister of Mary and Lazarus and a beloved follower of Jesus. c. AD 26–30 (Luke 10:38–42; John 11)

Mary, Martha's sister – Famous for worshiping at the feet of Jesus and anointing him with exotic perfume. c. AD 26–30 (Luke 10:38–42; John 11; 12:1–3)

Mary Magdalene – A demon-possessed woman who was delivered by Jesus, became his faithful follower, and was the first witness of his resurrection. c. AD 26–30 (Luke 8:2; John 20)

Melchizedek – The king and high priest of Salem to whom Abraham gave one-tenth of his spoils of war and who prefigured the later ministry of Jesus Christ. c. 2100 BC (Genesis 14; Psalm 110:4; Hebrews 5–7)

Methuseleh – The man who lived longer than anyone else, 969 years. Dates unknown (Genesis 5:27)

Miriam – Moses' older sister, a prophetess who helped her brothers lead Israel in the wilderness. c. 1526–1406 BC (Exodus 2; 15:20–21; Numbers 12; Micah 6:4)

Mordecai – Queen Esther's relative and surrogate father who helped her save the Jews from genocide. c. 478 BC (book of Esther)

Naaman – The military leader of Aram healed of leprosy by the prophet Elisha. c. 840 BC (2 Kings 5)

Naomi – The mother-in-law of Ruth and great-great-grandmother of King David. Dates unknown; Sometime during the era of judges: c. 1350–1050 BC (book of Ruth)

Nathan – The prophet who advised David and confronted him regarding David's sin with Bathsheba. c. 990–957 BC (2 Samuel 7:1–17; 12)

Nebuchadnezzar – The king of the neo-Babylonian Empire, whom Daniel served. c. 604–562 BC (2 Kings 24–25; 2 Chronicles 36; Jeremiah 24–39; Daniel 1–5)

Philemon – Received a letter from Paul urging him to forgive and restore his runaway slave who had converted to Christ. c. AD 60–62 (book of Philemon)

Philip – Led his friend Nathanael to Christ and was

Jesus' 12 Disciples

Peter
James, son of Zebedee
John
Andrew
Philip
Bartholomew (Nathanael)
Matthew (Levi)
Thomas
James, son of Alphaeus
Thaddaeus
Simon the Zealot
Judas Iscariot

handpicked by Jesus to be a disciple. c. AD 26–30 (Matthew 10:3; John 1:43–48; 6:5–7; 12:21–22; 14:8–9)

Pilate – The Roman governor whom the Jewish leaders pressured to sentence Jesus to death. c. AD 26–36 (Matthew 27:2, 15–26)

Priscilla and Aquila – A married couple, tentmakers by trade, who became close friends and ministry associates of Paul. c. AD 49–51 (Acts 18; Romans 16:3; 1 Corinthians 16:19; 2 Timothy 4:19)

Rachel – Sister of Leah; the favorite wife of Jacob and the mother of Joseph and Benjamin. c. 2005–1859 BC (Genesis 29–35)

Rahab – The prostitute in Jericho who saved two Israelite spies and is included in the genealogy of Jesus. c. 1406 BC (Joshua 2, 6; Matthew 1:5; Hebrews 11:31; James 2:25)

Rebekah – The wife of Isaac and the mother of Esau and Jacob. c. 2026 BC (Genesis 24–27)

Samson – Israel's judge with colossal physical strength and a weakness for pretty women. Dates unknown; sometime during the era of judges: c. 1350–1050 BC (Judges 13–16; Hebrews 11:32)

Silas – A faithful traveling companion and ministry partner of the apostle Paul. c. AD 49–51 (Acts 15–18)

Simeon – A godly aged Jewish man who recognized Jesus as the Messiah when Jesus was presented at the temple as an infant. c. 4 BC (Luke 2:25–35)

Simon the Zealot – One of Jesus' twelve disciples, identified as a member of the Zealots—a Jewish group of hardline revolutionaries. c. AD 26–30 (Matthew 10:4; Mark 3:18; Luke 6:15; Acts 1:13)

Stephen – One of the original deacons of the early church, an evangelist, and the first martyr. c. AD 30–32 (Acts 6–8)

Tamar – A widow who devised a plan to become pregnant by her father-in-law, Judah (one of Jacob's twelve sons), and became an ancestor of Jesus through their son Perez. c. 1880 BC (Genesis 38; Ruth 4:12; Matthew 1:3)

Thaddaeus – One of Jesus' twelve disciples; also called Judas (not Iscariot). c. AD 26 (Matthew 10:3; Mark 3:18; John 14:22)

Thomas – Known as the doubting disciple who worshiped Jesus as God when he saw him after the resurrection. c. AD 26–30 (Matthew 10:3; John 11:16; 14:5; 20:24–28)

Timothy – The son of a Jewish mother and Greek father who became one of Paul's most trusted young protégés and a pastor in the early church. c. AD 40s–60s (Acts 16–20; 1 Corinthians 4:17; 16:10; Philippians 2:19; 1 Thessalonians 3:1–6; 1 and 2 Timothy)

Titus – A pastor in the early church (at Crete) who was mentored by Paul. c. AD 40s–60s (2 Corinthians 2:13; 7–8; Galatians 2:1–3; book of Titus)

Uzziah (a.k.a. Azariah) – A king of Judah who honored God early in his reign but became prideful and was stricken with leprosy late in life. c. 792–740 BC (2 Chronicles 26)

Zacchaeus – A "vertically challenged," dishonest tax collector from Jericho who climbed a sycamore fig tree to see and hear Jesus and whose life was forever changed. c. AD 30 (Luke 19:1–10)

Zechariah – Elderly priest and husband of Elizabeth; was told by an angel that his wife would give birth to a special child (John the Baptist, the forerunner of Messiah). c. 5 BC (Luke 1)

Zerubbabel – A political leader who led the first of three groups of Jews returning to Jerusalem from Babylonian captivity. c. 538–516 BC (Ezra 2–5; Haggai 1–2)

ANOTHER JAMES?

The New Testament includes five men named James:

James #1: The apostle James, son of Zebedee and brother of John. Since the brothers are referred to as "James and John" in all but one place, James may have been the older brother. Along with Peter and John, this James was part of Jesus' inner circle. He was the first of the twelve disciples to die as a martyr (Acts 12:1–2).

James #2: The son of Alphaeus, he was one of the original twelve disciples. The Bible mentions him four times (Matthew 10:3; Mark 3:18; Luke 6:15; Acts 1:13).

James #3: This James appears in the Bible only to clarify the identity of the other disciple named Judas (not Judas Iscariot). The reference "Judas son of James" signifies this James as the *father* of a disciple, not as one of the twelve disciples himself (Luke 6:16; Acts 1:13).

James #4: This is Jesus' half brother who wrote the book of James. He became a leader in the early church after seeing the resurrected Christ (1 Corinthians 15:7). We read about him in Matthew 13:55, Mark 6:3, the book of James, and Acts 15:13–21.

James #5: The Bible mentions a fifth James in order to clarify the identity of a woman named Mary (a name many women share in the New Testament): "Mary the mother of James the younger" (Mark 15:40). Traditionally referred to as "James the Less" or "James the Younger" probably due to his age or his size. This James could be a reference to James #2, but we don't know for sure.

EXPLORING THE CONTENT: A BREAKDOWN OF BIBLE BOOKS

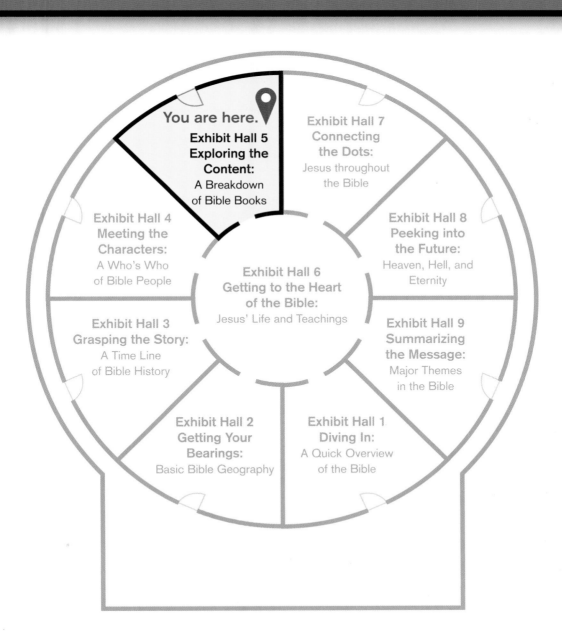

You are here.

**Exhibit Hall 5
Exploring the
Content:**
A Breakdown
of Bible Books

**Exhibit Hall 4
Meeting the
Characters:**
A Who's Who
of Bible People

**Exhibit Hall 3
Grasping the Story:**
A Time Line
of Bible History

**Exhibit Hall 2
Getting Your
Bearings:**
Basic Bible Geography

**Exhibit Hall 1
Diving In:**
A Quick Overview
of the Bible

**Exhibit Hall 6
Getting to the Heart
of the Bible:**
Jesus' Life and Teachings

**Exhibit Hall 7
Connecting
the Dots:**
Jesus throughout
the Bible

**Exhibit Hall 8
Peeking into
the Future:**
Heaven, Hell, and
Eternity

**Exhibit Hall 9
Summarizing
the Message:**
Major Themes
in the Bible

Want a concise summary of what each book of the Bible is about? You're in the right place! In this portion of your *Self-Guided Tour of the Bible*, you'll find a helpful overview of each of the Bible's sixty-six books.

Let's look at these books in brief: when and where the events described occurred, who the main characters are, what transpired, why the book is worth reading, a fascinating fact and one famous *verse* from each book. For simplicity's sake, we'll cover them in the order they appear in the Bible.

Old Testament

The first part of the Bible, the Old Testament, contains thirty-nine books. The Old Testament is divided into three broad categories:

- 17 history books
- 5 poetry/wisdom books
- 17 prophecy books (The first five are the *major prophets* and the remaining dozen shorter books are the *minor prophets*.)

Bible Fact

The first five books of the Old Testament are called the *Pentateuch*, from two Greek words: *penta*, meaning "five," and *teukos*, meaning "scroll." These books are also known as the Torah or the Law of Moses because it's believed that Moses authored these works.

 **THE HISTORY BOOKS**

Exhibit Hall 5

GENESIS

The beginning of the great story of God and his chosen people

When? Beginning of the world through c. 1805 BC (*c.* = approximate date)

Where? Mesopotamia, Canaan, Egypt

Who? Adam and Eve, Noah, Abraham and Sarah, Isaac, Jacob, Joseph

What? Genesis first highlights the events of creation, Adam and Eve's rebellion against God, and the great flood in which only Noah and his family are spared. Then the book focuses on God's choice of Abraham and Sarah, an elderly couple. He calls Abraham to go to Canaan and further promises to bless him and his descendants—and *to bless the world through him.*

Really? The Bible never states what kind of forbidden fruit Adam and Eve ate.

Why? Read Genesis for an understanding of how the world began, how it got "broken," and what God began to do about it.

Famous Verse: "In the beginning God created the heavens and the earth." —Genesis 1:1

Adam and Eve expelled from the Garden of Eden

EXODUS

God rescues his people from slavery in Egypt.

When? c. 1526–1446 BC

Where? Egypt, Sinai

Who? Moses, Pharaoh, Aaron

What? Abraham's descendants are enslaved in Egypt, and God calls Moses to liberate them. After a series of ten terrible judgments, Pharaoh (Egypt's king) reluctantly agrees to let the people go. Moses leads the twelve tribes of Israelites through the miraculous parting of the Red Sea to Mount Sinai, where they receive God's commandments and vow to be God's people.

Really? It's estimated by many scholars that the twelve tribes consisted of two to three million Israelites.

Why? Read Exodus to see God's supremacy over all other so-called gods and his mighty ability to save.

Famous Verse: "The LORD, the God of Israel, says: 'Let my people go.'" —Exodus 5:1

Sinai Desert and the Red Sea

LEVITICUS

A holy God calls his chosen people to be holy.

When? c. 1446 BC

Where? Sinai

Who? Moses, Aaron

What? Camped between their past (Egypt) and their future (Canaan), the Israelites receive detailed instructions for how unholy people must live with a holy God: Sin requires sacrifice. The sacrifices were to be repeated continuously, since people continued to sin.

Really? The word *holy* is found nearly sixty times in the twenty-seven chapters of Leviticus.

Why? Read Leviticus to see the holiness of God and the seriousness of sin, and to appreciate the once-for-all sacrifice made by Christ centuries later.

Famous Verse: "Therefore be holy, because I am holy." —Leviticus 11:45

NUMBERS

A two-week trip turns into a four-decade parade of dusty funerals.

When? c. 1446–1406 BC

Where? The wilderness south of Canaan

Who? Moses, Aaron

What? After a census, the Israelites set out from Sinai for the Promised Land of Canaan. But at the border, their fear of the Canaanites overshadows their faith in God. When they balk at going into the land, God decrees that they will wander in the desert until that unbelieving generation dies out.

Really? If 1.2 million Israelites age 20 and older died in the wilderness during the 40 years of wandering, that comes to about 82 funerals a day!

Why? Read Numbers to see the devastating consequences of unbelief as well as the mercy of God to ungrateful, undeserving people.

Famous Verse: "The LORD is slow to anger, abounding in love and forgiving sin and rebellion. Yet he does not leave the guilty unpunished." —Numbers 14:18

DEUTERONOMY

Moses teaches God's law to the next generation.

When? c. 1406 BC

Where? Moab (across the Jordan River and east of Canaan)

Who? Moses

What? Moses gives a farewell address to the younger generation of Israelites preparing to enter Canaan. *Deuteronomy* means "second law." Moses recaps the history of God's people and the laws God expects them to live by. The book ends with Moses' death.

Really? In Deuteronomy 24:5, newlyweds are commanded to honeymoon for a full year!

Why? Read Deuteronomy for a great reminder of God's faithfulness and why we need to love and cling to him.

Famous Verse: "Love the LORD your God with all your heart and with all your soul and with all your strength." —Deuteronomy 6:5

10 Commandments

The Ten Commandments are found in
Exodus 20:1–17 and Deuteronomy 5:5–21.

1. You shall have no other gods before me.

2. You shall not make for yourself an image. . . . You shall not bow down to them or worship them.

3. You shall not misuse the name of the Lord your God.

4. Remember the Sabbath day by keeping it holy.

5. Honor your father and your mother.

6. You shall not murder.

7. You shall not commit adultery.

8. You shall not steal.

9. You shall not give false testimony against your neighbor.

10. You shall not covet . . . anything that belongs to your neighbor.

JOSHUA

The Israelites inhabit the land God promised Abraham centuries before.

When? c. 1406–1350 BC

Where? Canaan

Who? Joshua, Rahab

What? Joshua leads the Israelites in conquering the key cities of the Promised Land and then in dividing and settling the land. Before dying at the age of 110, Joshua gives the nation a stirring farewell address.

Really? Joshua places a curse on any person who would attempt to rebuild the city of Jericho—that person's sons would die (Joshua 6:26). See the fulfillment of this curse in 1 Kings 16:34.

Why? Read Joshua for a great reminder of God's faithfulness and to see the rewards of faith.

Famous Verse: "Choose for yourselves this day whom you will serve. . . . But as for me and my household, we will serve the LORD." —Joshua 24:15

Joshua and the ark of the covenant crossing the Jordan River

Exhibit Hall 5

JUDGES

The Israelites fall into a repetitive cycle of sin, oppression, repentance, deliverance, and peace.

When? c. 1350–1050 BC

Where? Canaan

Who? Deborah, Gideon, Samson (and Delilah)—plus other judges

What? For a few hundred years after Joshua, a series of judges informally govern Israel. These are primarily military deliverers, not judicial leaders. God calls the judges into power when and where needed.

Really? In Judges 10:1, we read about a man named "Dodo."

Why? Read Judges for a powerful reminder of why we should remain loyal to God.

Famous Verse: "In those days Israel had no king; everyone did as they saw fit." —Judges 21:25

Judge	Meaning of Name	Scripture Reference
OTHNIEL	Lion of God	Judges 1:12–14; 3:7–11
EHUD	Strong	Judges 3:12–30
SHAMGAR	Cupbearer	Judges 3:31
DEBORAH	Bee	Judges 4:1–5:31
GIDEON	A cutting down	Judges 6:1–8:32
TOLA	Scarlet	Judges 10:1–2
JAIR	The Lord enlightens	Judges 10:3–5
JEPHTHAH	He opens	Judges 10:6–12:7
IBZAN	Splendid	Judges 12:8–10
ELON	Oak	Judges 12:11–12
ABDON	Service	Judges 12:13–15
SAMSON	Distinguished (or sun)	Judges 13:1–16:31

RUTH

A story of hope set against the dark backdrop of the time of the judges.

When? Dates unknown (sometime during the era of judges: c. 1350–1051 BC)

Where? Moab, Bethlehem

Who? Ruth, Naomi, Boaz

What? Widowed and penniless in Moab, Naomi returns to her hometown of Bethlehem with Ruth, her widowed daughter-in-law from Moab whose devotion to Naomi is unyielding.

In Bethlehem, they find help from a compassionate man named Boaz. As a close relative, he serves as a family redeemer ("kinsman-redeemer" or "guardian-redeemer") and buys Naomi's land for her and then marries Ruth. Centuries later, Jesus—a descendant of Boaz and Ruth—will serve as the ultimate Redeemer.

Really? Real estate deals were finalized in ancient Israel by having one of the parties take off his sandal and give it to the other (Ruth 4:7–8).

Why? Read Ruth to see a sparkling example of love and devotion in a decadent culture.

Famous Verse: "Your people will be my people and your God my God." —Ruth 1:16

Ruth in the wheat fields in Bethlehem

Exhibit Hall 5

1 SAMUEL

The prophet Samuel anoints Israel's first two kings.

When? c. 1100–1011 BC

Where? Israel

Who? Samuel, Saul, David

Samuel anoints David

What? At the end of the tumultuous period of the judges, the people of Israel clamor for a king. The prophet Samuel anoints Saul as Israel's first king. When Saul disobeys God, Samuel anoints David to lead the nation, though it is years before David assumes the throne.

Really? As a young man, David defeated in battle a warrior named Goliath who was over 9 feet (almost 3 m) tall (1 Samuel 17:4).

Why? Read 1 Samuel to see a sharp contrast between a king with little heart for God and one with great spiritual devotion.

Famous Verse: "People look at the outward appearance, but the LORD looks at the heart." —1 Samuel 16:7

TIME LINE OF THE LIFE OF DAVID

- In secret and at God's directive, Samuel anoints a young shepherd named David as king.

- David kills a giant named Goliath in battle.

- King Saul becomes jealous of David's success.

- Saul's son Jonathan declares lifelong friendship with David.

- David marries King Saul's daughter Michal.

- In jealousy, Saul tries to kill David, so David flees into exile.

- As an outlaw, David gathers a band of fighters and they attack Israel's enemies.

- David marries two women: Abigail and Ahinoam.

- Not long after Samuel's death, King Saul and Jonathan both are killed in battle.

2 SAMUEL

The story of King David, a very flawed man, but nevertheless, a man after God's own heart

When? c. 1011–971 BC

Where? Israel

Who? David, Bathsheba, Nathan

What? Following the death of Saul, David assumes the throne. Despite great military and political success, David is guilty of a great moral failure (adultery with Bathsheba and the murder of her husband, Uriah), causing long-term family problems and national strife.

Really? Benaiah is one of only three people in the Bible who killed a lion (2 Samuel 23:20). The others were Samson and David (Judges 14:5–9; 1 Samuel 17:34–36).

Why? Read 2 Samuel to see the dangers of spiritual complacency and the sobering consequences of sin, even when God is gracious.

Famous Verse: "David said to Nathan, 'I have sinned against the LORD.'" —2 Samuel 12:13

- David is officially made king of Israel at age 30.
- David takes more wives and has many children.
- David conquers Jerusalem and makes it his capital city.
- David sins by taking Bathsheba and arranging for her husband Uriah to be killed.
- He repents, but the child he and Bathsheba had dies.
- David and Bathsheba have another child together–a son, Solomon.
- David's family and kingdom experience incidents of severe strife and violence.
- David dies of natural causes and leaves his kingdom to Solomon.

1 KINGS

King Solomon's rise to power and the kingdom's subsequent split

When? c. 971–853 BC

Where? Israel, Judah

Who? Solomon, Elijah, Elisha

What? David's son Solomon assumes the throne and receives great wisdom from God. He builds the temple and enjoys a peaceful and prosperous reign—until he allows his appetite for many wives and their gods to corrupt his heart and mind. Following his death, the kingdom splits between the ten northern and the two southern tribes.

Really? At the dedication of the temple, 22,000 cattle and 120,000 sheep and goats were sacrificed (1 Kings 8:62–63).

Why? Read 1 Kings to see how someone as wise as Solomon can fall to temptation when placing other priorities ahead of devotion to God.

Famous Verse: "Observe what the LORD your God requires: Walk in obedience to him, and keep his decrees and commands." —1 Kings 2:3

2 KINGS

The decline and fall of Israel and Judah

When? c. 853–586 BC

Where? Israel, Judah

Who? Uzziah, Hezekiah, Josiah, and other kings; Elijah, Elisha

What? A parade of ungodly kings leads the northern kingdom of Israel to its destruction in 722 BC by Assyria. In the southern kingdom of Judah, a few godly kings are able to occasionally lead the nation back to God. But in 586 BC, Jerusalem is destroyed and Judah goes into Babylonian exile.

Really? A charioteer named Jehu is portrayed as the first reckless driver (2 Kings 9:20).

Why? Read 2 Kings to see why obedience matters and how to exert a positive influence.

Famous Verse: "Elijah went up to heaven in a whirlwind." —2 Kings 2:11

1 CHRONICLES

A retelling of the history of Israel, focusing on the reign of King David

When? c. 1011–971 BC

Where? Israel, Judah

Who? David

What? This review of Israel's history (beginning with nine chapters of genealogy) repeats many of the events of 2 Samuel, but it is written more from a priestly perspective—and likely written after the period of exile to encourage the people returning from exile.

Really? Our word *angel* comes from a Greek word used to translate the Hebrew word *malach* (for example, 1 Chron. 21:12–16). Both the Hebrew and Greek words mean "messenger."

Why? Read 1 Chronicles to be encouraged that God is faithful to his people and promises.

Famous Verse: "Jabez cried out to the God of Israel, 'Oh, that you would bless me and enlarge my territory!'" —1 Chronicles 4:10

2 CHRONICLES

A recounting of the history of Solomon's reign and the southern kingdom of Judah after him

When? c. 971–538 BC

Where? Judah, Babylon

Who? Solomon and nineteen other kings

What? This commentary on Israel's history repeats many of the events of 1 and 2 Kings. Originally one book with 1 Chronicles, it too reflects a priestly perspective—and was intended to encourage the Jews who had returned from exile.

Really? King Uzziah loved the soil (i.e., gardening; 2 Chronicles 26:10).

Why? Read 2 Chronicles to see the delight of living for God and the danger of turning away from him.

Famous Verse: "If my people, who are called by my name, will humble themselves and pray and seek my face and turn from their wicked ways, then I will hear from heaven, and I will forgive their sin and will heal their land." —2 Chronicles 7:14

EZRA

An account of what happened when the Jews returned home after living in exile

When? c. 538–450 BC

Where? Babylon, Jerusalem

Who? Cyrus, Zerubbabel, Haggai, Zechariah, Darius, Ezra

What? Following the decree of King Cyrus of Persia, the Jews begin returning to Jerusalem. The first group is led by a political leader named Zerubbabel and focuses on rebuilding the temple. Decades later, Ezra the priest leads another group back and sparks a revival.

Really? Ezra was a direct descendant of Moses' brother, Aaron (Ezra 7:1–5).

Why? Read Ezra to see God's faithfulness to his people and our need to be faithful to his Word.

Famous Verse: "And all the people gave a great shout of praise to the LORD, because the foundation of the house of the LORD was laid." —Ezra 3:11

NEHEMIAH

Rebuilding of the walls of Jerusalem

When? c. 445–432 BC

Where? Babylon, Jerusalem

Who? Nehemiah, Artaxerxes, Ezra

What? Nehemiah—a Jewish, high-ranking civil servant in Persia—returns to Jerusalem to lead the people in rebuilding the walls of Jerusalem in the face of much opposition.

Really? At the annual Festival of Tabernacles, the Israelites built little booths of sticks and branches and lived in them (Nehemiah 8:14–17). This festival was celebrated in Jesus' time and is still celebrated today as *Sukkot* (John 7:2).

Why? Read Nehemiah for powerful reminders of what is possible through trust in a big God.

Famous Verse: "The joy of the LORD is your strength." —Nehemiah 8:10

ESTHER

A young Jewish woman becomes queen of Persia and saves her people from annihilation.

When? c. 478 BC

Where? Susa in Persia

Who? Esther, Mordecai, King Xerxes, Haman

What? After she is selected by King Xerxes of Persia to be his queen, Esther is able to use her position to thwart a plot by Haman to wipe out her people.

Really? God's name is not mentioned in the book of Esther, but his power is evident in the events of the book.

Why? Read Esther for a vivid picture of how God works behind the scenes to orchestrate events to accomplish his purposes.

Famous Verse: "And who knows but that you have come to your royal position for such a time as this?" —Esther 4:14

Queen Esther denouncing Haman

THE POETRY/WISDOM BOOKS

JOB

A wealthy man of God loses everything except his faith.

When? Unknown, possibly c. 2100 BC

Where? Land of Uz (location unknown)

Who? Job, God, Satan, Job's friends

What? God allows Satan to test Job's devotion to God by taking Job's wealth, children, and health. Job's friends try to give reasons for his plight, but in the end God vindicates Job, criticizes his friends, and restores what Job lost.

Bible Fact

While Hebrew poetry doesn't rhyme, it does repeat words and phrases. It uses metaphor, irony, contrast, allegory, hyperbole, and intense language.

Really? Job 39:9–12 mentions some kind of untamable wild beast. Most Bible translations call the creature a "wild ox"; the KJV Bible translation calls it a "unicorn."

Why? Read Job for a vivid picture of how to trust God in the face of suffering, even when nothing makes sense.

Famous Verse: "The LORD gave and the LORD has taken away; may the name of the LORD be praised." —Job 1:21

Job and his friends grieving

PSALMS

A beloved collection of prayers and songs about God

When? Written c. 1410–450 BC

Where? Israel

Who? David and other writers

What? Israel's hymnbook, these 150 stand-alone compositions (about half written by David) include both individual and corporate laments, prayers of thanksgiving, hymns of praise, and songs of trust.

Really? The shortest chapter in the Bible is Psalm 117; the longest is two chapters later, Psalm 119.

Why? Read Psalms for how to worship God in good and bad times—and pray the psalms back to God!

Famous Verse: "Your word is a lamp for my feet, a light on my path." — Psalm 119:105

PSALM 23

Psalm 23 is one of the most beloved passages of the Bible. This beautiful poem speaks directly to the joys and fears we all have. It reminds us that the Lord is caring and compassionate. We, like sheep of the Great Shepherd, depend on his protection and provision.

The LORD is my shepherd;
  I shall not want.
He makes me to lie down in green pastures;
  He leads me beside the still waters.
He restores my soul;
  He leads me in the paths of righteousness
  For his name's sake.
Yea, though I walk through the valley of the
  shadow of death, I will fear no evil;
  For You are with me; Your rod and your staff,
  they comfort me.
You prepare a table before me in the presence of
  my enemies; You anoint my head with oil;
  My cup runs over.
Surely goodness and mercy shall follow me
  All the days of my life;
And I will dwell in the house of the LORD
  Forever.

—Psalm 23 NKJV

Exhibit Hall 5

PROVERBS

Collected sayings about the differences between foolish and wise living

When? Written c. 900s–700s BC

Where? Israel

Who? King Solomon (with contributions from Agur and Lemuel)

What? Beginning as a list of instructions to Solomon's son—whom Solomon doesn't name—the book unfolds with sound advice and truisms for all.

Really? Ants are praised twice in the book of Proverbs (6:6; 30:25).

Why? Read Proverbs for all sorts of practical insight on relationships, work, speech, and success in life.

Famous Verse: "Trust in the LORD with all your heart and lean not on your own understanding." —Proverbs 3:5

ECCLESIASTES

An honest look at the emptiness of life apart from God

When? Written c. 971–931 BC

Where? Israel

Who? "The Teacher, son of David, king in Jerusalem" (Ecclesiastes 1:1)

What? The world-weary, disillusioned author (King Solomon) reflects on the meaning and purpose of life.

Really? In the NIV Bible translation, the word *meaningless* is found over thirty times in the book of Ecclesiastes; other translations use the words *futile* or *vanity*.

Why? Read Ecclesiastes for a powerful reminder that a life apart from God is no life at all.

Famous Verse: "To every thing there is a season, and a time to every purpose under the heaven." —Ecclesiastes 3:1 KJV

SONG OF SONGS

A book of passionate love

When? Written c. 971–931 BC

Where? Israel

Who? The lover (Solomon) and his bride

What? Also called *Song of Solomon*, this passionate poem celebrates the beauty and joy of intimate, committed marital love. Some view the book as an allegory of Jesus and his church, with Jesus as the bridegroom and the church as his pure, spotless bride.

Really? Solomon's bride may have been from Lebanon (Song of Songs 4:8).

Why? Read Song of Songs to glimpse God's great gift of marital intimacy and affection.

Famous Verse: "Let his banner over me be love." —Song of Songs 2:4

Exhibit Hall 5

THE PROPHECY BOOKS

MAJOR PROPHETS

ISAIAH

A call to the southern kingdom of Judah to come back to God

When? c. 760–673 BC

Where? Judah

Who? Isaiah

> **Bible Fact**
>
> A *prophet* is a person chosen and gifted by God to urge people to live for God because of what God has done in the past or will do in the future. Biblical prophets repeated God's pronouncements from the past and/or revealed God's plans for the future.

What? The longest of all the prophecy books, Isaiah warns of imminent judgment and comforts his people with future hope. Both predictions come to pass. First, Babylon conquers and exiles the people of Judah. About seventy years after that, King Cyrus permits them to return home.

Really? The longest name in the Bible belongs to one of Isaiah's sons: Maher-Shalal-Hash-Baz which means "quick to the plunder" (Isaiah 8:1).

Why? Read Isaiah for an epic look at God's holiness, grace, and sovereign control of all things.

Famous Verse: "So do not fear, for I am with you; do not be dismayed, for I am your God." —Isaiah 41:10

The prophet Isaiah

JEREMIAH

A broken-hearted prophet tells hard-hearted Judah to turn from sin.

When? c. 626–582 BC

Where? Judah

Who? Jeremiah and multiple kings

What? Like Isaiah, Jeremiah warns the southern kingdom (its kings and people) of impending destruction at the hands of Babylon, seventy years of exile, and an eventual return to Judah.

Really? When Jeremiah began to prophesy, King Josiah was twenty-one and had already been reigning for thirteen years (2 Kings 22:1; Jeremiah 1:2).

Why? Read Jeremiah for a picture of what it means to speak hard truth with great love.

Famous Verse: "'For I know the plans I have for you,' declares the LORD, 'plans to prosper you and not to harm you, plans to give you hope and a future.'" —Jeremiah 29:11

LAMENTATIONS

Jeremiah's grief over the destruction of Jerusalem and the exile of his people

When? c. 586 BC

Where? Judah, Jerusalem

Who? Jeremiah

What? Writing in the form of funeral dirges, Jeremiah expresses great sorrow that Judah has fallen, the temple has been destroyed, and his people have been carried away into captivity.

Really? "Snow" is mentioned in Lamentations 4:7 and in over twenty other places in the Bible.

Why? Read Lamentations for a reminder that God grieves when his people sin and suffer.

Famous Verse: "For his compassions never fail. They are new every morning; great is your faithfulness." —Lamentations 3:22–23

EZEKIEL

Words of rebuke, calls to repent, visions to ponder, and messages of hope for God's exiled people

When? c. 593–571 BC

Where? Babylon

Who? Ezekiel, King Nebuchadnezzar of Babylon

What? The priest-turned-prophet shares messages of doom and hope—often via bizarre methods.

Really? Ezekiel wore a turban (Ezekiel 24:16–17).

Why? Read Ezekiel for a reminder that God does indeed work in mysterious ways.

Famous Verse: "I will remove from them their heart of stone and give them a heart of flesh." —Ezekiel 11:19

DANIEL

The remarkable life and strange visions of a Jewish prophet in Babylonian captivity

When? c. 605–535 BC

Where? Babylon

Who? Daniel, King Nebuchadnezzar of Babylon, Shadrach, Meshach, Abednego

What? Taken from Judah to Babylon and forced into King Nebuchadnezzar's service, Daniel demonstrates integrity. Via visions of the future, he reminds God's people that God is in control of history and that a Savior is coming.

Daniel in the lions' den

Really? Upon arriving in Babylon, Daniel, whose name means "God is my judge," was given the name Belteshazzar, which means "Bel [a Babylonian god] protects" (Daniel 1:7).

Why? Read Daniel to see that God's purposes and plans cannot be thwarted.

Famous Verse: "In my vision at night I looked, and there before me was one like a son of man, coming with the clouds of heaven." —Daniel 7:13

MINOR PROPHETS

The lives and ministries of the minor prophets cover more than 300 years and span many events in Jewish history. They appear in the Old Testament in this order: Hosea, Joel, Amos, Obadiah, Jonah, Micah, Nahum, Habakkuk, Zephaniah, Haggai, Zechariah, and Malachi. This chart puts the minor prophets in *chronological* order:

Prophet	Date	Details
JONAH	c. 783–753 BC	Preached, reluctantly, a message of repentance to the Assyrian capital of Nineveh. His story emphasizes God's love for all people.
AMOS	c. 760–753 BC	A shepherd/farmer-turned-prophet who called the affluent of the northern kingdom to repent.
HOSEA	c. 752–722 BC	A contemporary of Isaiah whose name means "salvation." He prophesied to the northern kingdom.
MICAH	c. 738–698 BC	His message: Judgment is coming, but so is the Messiah!
NAHUM	c. 663–612 BC	Because the revival under Jonah was short-lived, Nahum told of coming judgment on Assyria.
ZEPHANIAH	c. 641–628 BC	He announced judgment followed by restoration.
HABAKKUK	c. 609–598 BC	Wrestled with God's purposes of using an evil nation—Babylon—to judge Judah. He ultimately expressed trust in God.
OBADIAH	c. 586 BC	Wrote the shortest Old Testament book and announced coming judgment on the Edomites. About the same time, Judah, the southern kingdom, fell to Babylon.
HAGGAI	c. 520 BC	Called his countrymen to rebuild the temple, which happened under the leadership of Zerubbabel four years later in 516 BC.
ZECHARIAH	c. 520–518 BC	Called his people to finish the temple rebuilding project in light of the coming Messiah.
MALACHI	c. 400s BC	He confronted complacency and hard-heartedness among his people.
JOEL	Dates unknown	He prophesied to Judah using a locust plague as an object lesson.

HOSEA

A prophet's adulterous wife symbolizes national unfaithfulness.

When? c. 752–722 BC

Where? Northern kingdom of Israel

Who? Hosea, Gomer

Bible Fact

Twelve Old Testament prophets are referred to as the minor prophets. This doesn't mean their work is insignificant. It means they wrote shorter books compared to the major prophets.

What? God instructs his prophet Hosea to marry an unfaithful wife (Gomer) to illustrate how Israel has been cheating on God by pursuing false gods.

Really? Hosea's name means "salvation."

Why? Read Hosea to see that sin isn't just breaking God's law—it's breaking his heart.

Famous Verse: "For I desire mercy, not sacrifice, and acknowledgment of God rather than burnt offerings." —Hosea 6:6

JOEL

A locust plague pictures a worse judgment to come.

When? Unknown (possibly 609–586 BC or 515–350 BC)

Where? The southern kingdom of Judah

Who? Joel, the people of Judah

What? Joel warns his countrymen to stop sinning or face the terrible Day of the Lord.

Really? There are as many as thirteen different characters named "Joel" in the Bible.

Why? Read Joel to be reminded that God both judges sin and gives grace to repentant sinners.

Famous Verse: "And everyone who calls on the name of the LORD will be saved." —Joel 2:32; Acts 2:21

AMOS

Boldly confronting a prosperous, complacent, pseudo-religious culture

When? c. 760–753 BC

Where? The northern kingdom of Israel

Who? Amos, Amaziah

What? Amos is called by God to speak hard truth to those who were acting unjustly.

Really? Amos was a herdsman and farmer who grew sycamore figs (Amos 7:14).

Why? Read Amos to wake yourself up from spiritual apathy.

Famous Verse: "Let justice roll on like a river, righteousness like a never-failing stream!" —Amos 5:24

Sycamore figs

OBADIAH

The nation of Edom is condemned for mistreating God's chosen people.

When? c. 586 BC

Where? Jerusalem

Who? Obadiah and the nation of Edom

What? The prophet denounces the prideful Edomites and declares their doom for being hostile to the Israelites, their distant relatives.

Really? Obadiah is the shortest book in the Old Testament.

Why? Read Obadiah for a reminder that God judges those who persecute his people.

Famous Verse: "The pride of your heart has deceived you." —Obadiah 3

JONAH

A stubborn Jewish prophet needs divine convincing before preaching to the wicked Assyrians.

When? c. 783–753 BC

Where? Israel, Nineveh, Mediterranean Sea

Who? Jonah and the Ninevites

Jonah thrown overboard

What? In contrast to Christ who, centuries later, will have great compassion on the wicked and gladly preach God's message of repentance, Jonah resists his calling. But after God forces him to spend three days and nights in the belly of a large fish, Jonah relents and obeys God. God prevails in the end.

Really? Called to travel northeast 500 miles (805 km) to Nineveh in Assyria, Jonah instead tries to sail 2,500 miles (4,023 km) west to Tarshish.

Why? Read Jonah to see God's love and concern for all the nations of the world.

Famous Verse: "From inside the fish Jonah prayed to the LORD his God." —Jonah 2:1

MICAH

Seek justice, love mercy, walk humbly.

When? c. 738–698 BC

Where? Judah

Who? Micah and the people of God

What? Micah announces that God's people need to exchange their greed for humility.

Really? Christ's birth in Bethlehem is predicted in Micah 5:2, some seven centuries before the event.

Why? Read Micah for a reminder that God doesn't take disobedience lightly.

Famous Verse: "And what does the LORD require of you? To act justly and to love mercy and to walk humbly with your God." —Micah 6:8

NAHUM

Sinful nations reap what they sow.

When? c. 663–612 BC

Where? Assyria

Who? Nahum and the Assyrians

What? After a period of time after heeding Jonah's message to repent, the Assyrians return to their old ways of rebellion. God sends Nahum to announce doom for the nation.

Really? Nahum the prophet isn't mentioned anywhere else in the Bible.

Why? Read Nahum for a reminder that God is just and that no one gets away with anything.

Famous Verse: "The LORD is slow to anger but great in power; the LORD will not leave the guilty unpunished." —Nahum 1:3

HABAKKUK

We can trust God's heart, even when we don't understand his ways.

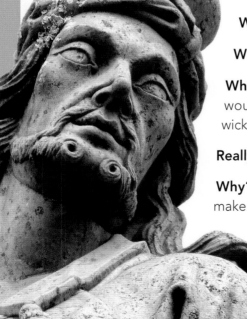

When? c. 609–598 BC

Where? Judah

Who? Habakkuk and the Babylonians

What? The prophet Habakkuk wrestles with why God would judge his wicked nation by using an even more wicked nation.

Really? The name *Habakkuk* might mean "embrace."

Why? Read Habakkuk when world events don't seem to make sense or things seem out of control.

Famous Verse: "For I am going to do something in your days that you would not believe, even if you were told." —Habakkuk 1:5

ZEPHANIAH

A wake-up call for a sleepy people

When? c. 641–628 BC

Where? Jerusalem

Who? The people of Judah

What? Like most of the prophets (and like the later New Testament message of the gospel), Zephaniah reminds people of God's judgment on sin and his grace and hope for sinners.

Really? Zephaniah 3:17 says that God "sings" over his people.

Why? Read Zephaniah to challenge spiritual indifference.

Famous Verse: "He will no longer rebuke you, but will rejoice over you with singing." —Zephaniah 3:17

HAGGAI

Finish rebuilding God's temple!

When? c. 520 BC

Where? Jerusalem

Who? Haggai, Zerubbabel, Joshua the high priest, the people of Judah

What? The people of Judah receive encouragement to complete the important task of building their place of worship.

Really? Haggai received four divine messages: three for Zerubbabel and one for the priests of the day.

Why? Read Haggai when you are struggling with priorities in life.

Famous Verse: "Give careful thought to your ways." —Haggai 1:5

Sounding the shofar

ZECHARIAH

Ditto what Haggai said!

When? c. 520–518 BC

Where? Jerusalem

Who? Zechariah, Zerubbabel, Joshua the high priest, the people of Judah

What? Like his fellow prophet Haggai, Zechariah challenges his countrymen to finish the temple. Why? Because the Messiah is coming!

Really? Zechariah's name means "the Lord remembers."

Why? Read Zechariah when your hope in a good future is fading.

Zechariah's first vision (Zechariah 1:8)

Famous Verse: "'Not by might nor by power, but by my Spirit,' says the LORD Almighty." —Zechariah 4:6

MALACHI

God woos and pursues his people when they are stagnant and stuck.

When? c. 400s BC

Where? Jerusalem

Who? Malachi and the priests

What? Malachi lovingly but firmly confronts his fellow Jews for letting their hearts grow cold and hard toward God.

Really? Malachi's four chapters bring the total number of Old Testament chapters to 929.

Why? Read Malachi when you sense yourself becoming spiritually apathetic.

Famous Verse: "Bring the whole tithe into the storehouse . . . and see if I will not throw open the floodgates of heaven and pour out so much blessing that there will not be room enough to store it." —Malachi 3:10

New Testament

The second part of the Bible, the New Testament, contains twenty-seven books. They're subdivided into three broad categories:

- 5 history books (the four Gospels, plus Acts)
- 21 epistles (letters)
- 1 prophecy book (Revelation)

The Four Gospels

The books of Matthew, Mark, Luke, and John are called the Four Gospels. They are written portraits of Jesus' life. Each author was writing to a different audience, so they focus on different things in Jesus' life.

Matthew's focus:
Jesus is the long-awaited Messiah—the Christ.

Mark's focus:
Jesus has a servant's heart for humanity.

Luke's focus:
Jesus is the perfect human being, our best example.

John's focus:
Jesus is the Son of God. Let us put our faith in him!

THE HISTORY BOOKS

MATTHEW

How Jesus fulfills the Old Testament prophecies of the Messiah

When? c. 4 BC–AD 30

Where? Israel (and a short time in Egypt)

Who? Jesus, Joseph, Mary, Herod the Great, John the Baptist, the twelve disciples

What? Matthew (a.k.a. Levi), originally a tax collector for the Roman government and later an apostle of Jesus, writes primarily to his fellow Jews to make the case that Jesus is the Messiah. Matthew focuses on Jesus' ministry—preaching about the kingdom of God, doing miracles, dying for sin, and rising from the dead. Matthew emphasizes Jesus' intentional efforts to make disciples whom he commissions to go and make other disciples all around the world.

Bible Fact

The biblical title *Messiah* (Christ in Greek) comes from a Hebrew word that means "anointed one." It refers ultimately to the great prophet/priest/king who would, as a descendant of King David, bring to earth a never-ending kingdom marked by righteousness and peace.

Really? The Gospel of Matthew contains some of the most well-known teachings of Jesus, including the Beatitudes (5:3–12), the Sermon on the Mount (chapters 5–7), and the Lord's Prayer (6:9–13).

Why? Read Matthew to see Jesus' credentials as the long-prophesied "king of the Jews" (2:2; 27:11)—and our King.

Famous Verse: "Therefore go and make disciples of all nations, baptizing them in the name of the Father and of the Son and of the Holy Spirit." —Matthew 28:19

MARK

How Jesus came to destroy evil and the works of the devil

When? c. AD 26–30

Where? Israel

Who? Jesus, John the Baptist, the twelve disciples, Pilate, the Jewish religious leaders

What? Mark (a.k.a. John Mark), a close companion of the apostle Peter and associate of Paul, seems to have written his Gospel to Roman Christians. This is the most action-packed of the four Gospels. It emphasizes the miracles and servant mind-set of Jesus.

Really? In Mark's sixteen chapters, the word *immediately* appears often—almost forty times in the NASB Bible translation!

Why? Read Mark, the shortest Gospel, for a vivid picture of how Jesus is our servant Savior.

Famous Verse: "For even the Son of Man did not come to be served, but to serve, and to give his life as a ransom for many." —Mark 10:45

LUKE

A Gentile doctor's biography of Jesus, the perfect man and Savior

When? c. 4 BC–AD 30

Where? Israel

Who? Elizabeth, Zechariah, John the Baptist, Mary, Joseph, Jesus, Herod the Great, the twelve disciples, the Jewish religious leaders

What? Luke emphasizes Jesus' compassion and love for people, the importance of prayer, the Holy Spirit, and Jesus' fair treatment of women—all in order to demonstrate Jesus' perfect humanity and his relentless mission "to seek and to save the lost" (Luke 19:10).

Really? Luke is the only Gospel writer to include details of Jesus sweating "drops of blood" on the night before his crucifixion (Luke 22:44). *Hematidrosis* is an actual medical term to describe when a person's blood is excreted through the skin due to extreme anguish.

Why? Read Luke for a scholarly and thorough account of the life of Jesus.

Famous Verse: "For the Son of Man came to seek and to save the lost." —Luke 19:10

JOHN

Jesus is fully God and fully man, and eternal life is found only in him.

When? c. AD 26–30

Where? Israel

Who? Jesus, John the Baptist, the twelve disciples, Mary, Martha, and Lazarus, Pilate, the Jewish religious leaders

What? Writing late in the first century, John—"the disciple whom Jesus loved" (John 13:23)—makes a compelling case for readers to trust "that Jesus is the Messiah, the Son of God, and that by believing you may have life in his name" (John 20:31).

Really? The shortest verse in the Bible is John 11:35: "Jesus wept."

Why? Read John for a unique and intimate perspective on Jesus from, arguably, his closest earthly friend.

Famous Verse: "For God so loved the world that he gave his one and only Son, that whoever believes in him shall not perish but have eternal life." —John 3:16

Jesus and the Samaritan woman (John 4)

135

ACTS

The Spirit-led activities of the apostles and the early church

When? c. AD 30–62

Where? "Jerusalem . . . Judea . . . Samaria . . . the ends of the earth" (Acts 1:8)

Who? The Holy Spirit, Peter, John, James, Stephen, Philip, Paul (Saul), Barnabas, Silas, Luke

What? Continuing the historical record he began in his Gospel, Luke gives an orderly account of the birth and growth of Christianity (despite much opposition) and the coming of the Holy Spirit, as promised by Jesus (John 16:5–15). The apostle Peter dominates chapters 1–12. The apostle Paul takes center stage in chapters 13–28. The book ends with Paul in prison in Rome. Often referred to as the "Acts of the Apostles," Luke's work could be more accurately titled the "Acts of the Holy Spirit in and through the Apostles."

Really? A man named Eutychus was sleeping and fell out an upstairs window to his death while Paul was preaching. Paul went downstairs and raised the man from the dead (Acts 20:9–12).

Why? Read Acts for an encouraging look at God's supernatural power to transform lives!

Famous Verse: "You will receive power when the Holy Spirit comes on you; and you will be my witnesses in Jerusalem, and in all Judea and Samaria, and to the ends of the earth." —Acts 1:8

Island of Crete in the Mediterranean Sea

 **THE EPISTLES**

ROMANS

The basics of Christian faith and living

When? c. AD 56–57

Where? To Rome from Paul in Corinth

Who? Paul, the church in Rome

What? Paul's theological masterpiece, this letter presents what Christians believe about sin and salvation, and how Christians should be living in light of those eternal truths.

> **Bible Fact**
>
> Twenty-one of the twenty-seven books of the New Testament are epistles (letters). Some are lengthy, others not much more than notes. Some were written to churches, others to individuals. The first thirteen of these letters were written by Paul, the rest by other church leaders.

Really? The great sixteenth-century reformer Martin Luther said the book of Romans "deserves not only to be known word for word by every Christian, but to be the subject of his meditation day by day, the daily bread of his soul."

Why? Read Romans whenever you lose sight of God's grace or question God's love.

Famous Verse: "We know that in all things God works for the good of those who love him, who have been called according to his purpose." —Romans 8:28

1 CORINTHIANS

Struggling to live purely in an impure world

When? c. AD 55–56

Where? To Corinth from Paul in Ephesus

Who? Paul, the immature believers in the church in Corinth

What? With forcefulness, Paul addresses divisions and immorality within the church in Corinth (an openly pagan city). Then he teaches how to worship God together and addresses questions about the resurrection of Christ.

Really? The Greeks created a verb from the name *Corinth* that meant to live a drunken and immoral lifestyle.

Why? Read 1 Corinthians to be reminded of why the great commandment to love God and love others is so important to follow.

Famous Verse: "Love is patient, love is kind. It does not envy, it does not boast, it is not proud." —1 Corinthians 13:4

2 CORINTHIANS

Paul defends his ministry from unfair attacks so that the gospel will not be discredited.

When? c. AD 56–57

Where? To Corinth from Paul in Philippi

Who? Paul, Timothy, Titus, the church in Corinth, false teachers

What? False teachers, who were infiltrating the Corinthian church, question Paul's authority. Paul writes to defend his position as a true apostle of Jesus Christ. He emphasizes how Christians who love Jesus will be willing to suffer for Jesus. Using himself as an example, Paul describes how he has embraced his own suffering for the sake of the gospel.

Really? In Paul's day, Corinth was the most modern and industrious city in Greece.

Why? Read 2 Corinthians to see the importance of living *by* God's truth and living *with* integrity in an evil world.

Famous Verse: "For Christ's sake, I delight in weaknesses, in insults, in hardships, in persecutions, in difficulties. For when I am weak, then I am strong." —2 Corinthians 12:10

GALATIANS

Religious efforts are not what make us right with God.

When? c. AD 49

Where? To Asia Minor (Galatia) from Paul (location unknown)

Who? Paul, Timothy, Titus, the churches in Galatia, false teachers

What? When some Jewish teachers begin disputing Paul's message and discrediting his ministry, he writes a strong letter to say that we are saved by God's grace alone through our faith alone—and not by anything we do.

Really? After meeting the resurrected Christ, Paul went to Arabia for about three years (Galatians 1:17–18).

Why? Read Galatians when you start feeling like it's up to you to earn God's approval.

Famous Verse: "The fruit of the Spirit is love, joy, peace, forbearance, kindness, goodness, faithfulness, gentleness and self-control." —Galatians 5:22–23

EPHESIANS

A look at all that God has done for us in Christ

When? c. AD 60–62

Where? To Ephesus from Paul in Rome

Who? Paul, the church in Ephesus

What? This compact letter shows the riches Christians have *in Christ* and the responsibilities believers have in living *for Christ*.

Really? The archaeological ruins at Ephesus (in modern-day Turkey) are some of the best-preserved sites from Bible times.

Why? Read Ephesians to strengthen your faith and spark growth in your life.

Famous Verse: "For it is by grace you have been saved, through faith—and this is not from yourselves, it is the gift of God." —Ephesians 2:8

PHILIPPIANS

A joyful thank-you note from the imprisoned Paul

When? c. AD 60–61

Where? To Philippi from Paul in Rome

Who? Paul, the church in Philippi

What? Paul writes from his cell in Rome to express gratitude for a financial gift. In the process he exudes joy and urges the believers in Greece to live humbly and in unity—in short, to press on to know Christ better and better.

Really? Paul was jailed when he visited Philippi (Acts 16:23). Later when he wrote to the Philippians, he was in jail in Rome!

Why? Read Philippians when you are struggling to be content.

Famous Verse: "I can do all things through Christ who strengthens me." —Philippians 4:13 NKJV

COLOSSIANS

The supremacy of Jesus over everything and everyone else

When? c. AD 60–61

Where? To Colossae from Paul in Rome

Who? Paul, Timothy, Tychicus, Mark, Epaphras, the church in Colossae

What? In the face of teachings that rejected Jesus as God in the flesh, Paul passionately champions Jesus' deity (i.e., that Jesus was fully man and fully God) and emphasizes that Jesus alone was able to save humankind from sin through his death on the cross.

Really? It appears that certain Colossians were involved in some form of angel worship (Colossians 2:18).

Why? Read Colossians when you feel spiritually distracted or confused.

Famous Verse: "Whatever you do, work at it with all your heart, as working for the Lord, not for human masters." —Colossians 3:23

Exhibit Hall 5

1 THESSALONIANS

Maturing in faith and understanding the second coming of Jesus

When? c. AD 50–52

Where? To Thessalonica from Paul in Corinth

Who? Paul, Silas, Timothy, the church in Thessalonica

What? Because the Thessalonian believers were young in the faith, experiencing persecution, and confused about the return of Jesus, Paul wrote to encourage and instruct them.

Really? Paul wrote the most books of the New Testament (thirteen epistles), but Luke wrote more words in his two books—Luke and Acts.

Why? Read 1 Thessalonians when you feel shaky in your faith.

Famous Verse: "Pray without ceasing, in everything give thanks." —1 Thessalonians 5:17–18 NKJV

2 THESSALONIANS

More about Christ's return

When? c. AD 52

Where? To Thessalonica from Paul in Corinth

Who? Paul, Silas, Timothy, the church in Thessalonica

What? Paul writes a second, and even shorter, letter to the church in Thessalonica to clear up some misunderstandings about Jesus' second coming and to encourage believers not to give up during times of difficulty.

Really? Paul alone uses the terms "man of lawlessness" and "lawless one" to describe an evil leader (possibly the antichrist) whom Jesus will defeat after Jesus' second coming (2 Thessalonians 2:3, 8–9).

Why? Read 2 Thessalonians when you feel complacent in your faith.

Famous Verse: "As for you, brothers and sisters, never tire of doing what is good." —2 Thessalonians 3:13

1 TIMOTHY

Encouragement for a young pastor

When? c. AD 62–66

Where? To Ephesus from Paul in Rome

Who? Paul, Timothy

What? The wise and experienced Paul offers counsel and encouragement to his sometimes-timid protégé Timothy.

Really? Timothy's mother was Jewish and his father was Greek (Acts 16:1).

Why? Read 1 Timothy for a crash course in leadership.

Famous Verse: "The love of money is a root of all kinds of evil." —1 Timothy 6:10

2 TIMOTHY

Last words from a giant in the faith

When? c. AD 66–67

Where? To Ephesus from Paul in Rome

Who? Paul, Timothy

What? Paul offers a final, personal challenge for Timothy to stand firm, preach God's Word, and fight "the good fight" of faith (2 Timothy 4:7).

Really? Tradition says that Paul was martyred shortly after writing this letter.

Why? Read 2 Timothy for a reminder of the things that matter most.

Famous Verse: "God has not given us a spirit of fear, but of power and of love and of a sound mind." —2 Timothy 1:7 NKJV

The apostle Paul

TITUS

A manual for churches

When? c. AD 64–66

Where? To Crete from Paul in Rome

Who? Paul, Titus

What? Paul lists the characteristics and qualities of godly leaders in the church and godly Christians in the world.

Really? The only lawyers mentioned by name in the Bible are Zenas (Titus 3:13) and Tertullus (Acts 24:1).

Why? Read Titus to see what God expects of spiritual leaders (and followers).

Famous Verse: "In everything set them an example by doing what is good." —Titus 2:7

PHILEMON

Paul asks Philemon to forgive Onesimus.

When? c. AD 60–62

Where? To Colossae from Paul in Rome

Who? Paul, Onesimus, Philemon

What? Paul sends Onesimus—a runaway slave and new Christian—home, appealing to his master, Philemon, to receive him as a new brother in Christ.

Really? As the owner of a fugitive slave, Philemon had the legal right to have Onesimus killed.

Why? Read Philemon to see the reconciling power of the gospel.

Famous Verse: "Perhaps the reason he was separated from you for a little while was that you might have him back forever—no longer as a slave, but better than a slave, as a dear brother." —Philemon 15–16

HEBREWS

Christ is greater!

When? c. AD 60–69

Where? Location unknown

Who? Jewish Christians

What? When young Jewish believers in Christ are tempted to forsake the gospel and return to their Jewish religion, the unnamed author of the book of Hebrews shows them how Christ is superior to everything about their former religion: angels, Moses, the Old Testament priesthood, the sacrificial system, and the old covenant.

Really? Speculation for who wrote Hebrews includes Paul, Barnabas, Apollos, and Priscilla.

Why? Read Hebrews to see the difference between a life of faith and a life of religious effort.

Famous Verse: "Now faith is confidence in what we hope for and assurance about what we do not see." —Hebrews 11:1

JAMES

Balancing faith with action

When? c. AD 49

Where? Location unknown

Who? James (the half brother of Jesus), Jewish Christians "scattered among the nations" (James 1:1)

What? Reminiscent of Proverbs, James writes a pithy, concise letter to urge those who say they believe in God's Word to "do what it says" (James 1:22).

Really? The command "love your neighbor" (James 2:8) is found eight other times in the New Testament.

Why? Read James when your faith is more a noun than a verb.

Famous Verse: "As the body without the spirit is dead, so faith without deeds is dead." —James 2:26

1 PETER

Encouragement for suffering believers

When? c. AD 64–65

Where? To Asia Minor from Peter in Rome

Who? Peter, Mark, Christians in Asia Minor

What? Peter encourages believers to persevere during suffering and to live holy lives because Jesus will one day return.

Really? Peter identifies the place where he writes this letter as "Babylon" (1 Peter 5:13). This may refer to a city named Babylon, or it may metaphorically refer to Rome.

Why? Read 1 Peter when you are belittled or maligned for your faith.

Famous Verse: "Cast all your anxiety on him because he cares for you." —1 Peter 5:7

2 PETER

Beware of false teaching!

When? c. AD 64–65

Where? To Asia Minor from Peter in Rome

Who? Peter, Paul, Christians in Asia Minor

What? In his first letter, Peter warned about persecution from outside the church. Here he warns about unbiblical thinking and teaching within the church.

Really? Tradition says Peter was martyred for his faith by being crucified upside down.

Why? Read 2 Peter when you hear strange ideas about the Christian faith.

Famous Verse: "His divine power has given us everything we need for a godly life through our knowledge of him who called us by his own glory and goodness." —2 Peter 1:3

The apostle Peter

1 JOHN

Remaining in the love of Christ

When? c. AD 85–96

Where? To Asia Minor from John in Ephesus

Who? John, Christians in Asia Minor

What? An aging apostle wisely urges young believers to avoid sin, watch for error, live in love, and find assurance in God's free gift of eternal life.

Really? It's believed that the apostle John was the only one of Jesus' apostles (excluding Judas) who did not die a martyr's death.

Why? Read 1 John when you need a reminder to "walk the talk" of the Christian life.

Famous Verse: "If we confess our sins, he is faithful and just and will forgive us our sins and purify us from all unrighteousness." —1 John 1:9

The apostle John

2 JOHN

Not all "truths" are true.

When? c. AD 85–96

Where? To Asia Minor from John in Ephesus

Who? John, "the lady chosen by God and . . . her children" (2 John 1); believers in Asia Minor and all Christians everywhere

What? The shortest book in the Bible has a short, twofold message: Love one another and look out for religious scammers!

Really? John wrote a little over 20 percent of the New Testament (five out of the twenty-seven books).

Why? Read 2 John for a challenge to walk in love and in truth.

Famous Verse: "This is love: that we walk in obedience to his commands." —2 John 6

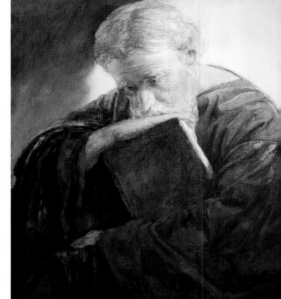

3 JOHN

How to treat people

When? c. AD 85–96

Where? To Asia Minor from John in Ephesus

Who? John, Gaius, Diotrephes, Christians in Asia Minor

What? John praises Gaius for his hospitality and rebukes Diotrephes for his pride.

Really? Third John is one of only four New Testament books that doesn't use the word *grace*. The others are Matthew, Mark, and 1 John.

Why? Read 3 John for insight in how to treat Christian workers.

Famous Verse: "We ought therefore to show hospitality to such people so that we may work together for the truth." —3 John 8

JUDE

Be on guard against deceivers.

When? c. AD 60s–80s (exact date unknown)

Where? Location unknown

Who? Jude, James

What? Jude offers a sobering warning to be discerning about the teaching we hear.

Really? Jesus' half brother Judas, the likely author of this book, was also known as Jude, possibly to differentiate him from the traitor Judas Iscariot (Matthew 13:55; Mark 6:3).

Why? Read Jude to see the importance of right beliefs.

Famous Verse: "Keep yourselves in God's love as you wait for the mercy of our Lord Jesus Christ to bring you to eternal life." —Jude 21

PROPHECY BOOK

Though multiple New Testament books feature prophetic passages, Revelation is the one book that is almost exclusively *apocalyptic*. Apocalyptic writings reveal God's plans and coming events through signs, symbols, and visions.

REVELATION

Jesus gives John a grand vision of the future.

When? c. AD 85–96

Where? To Asia Minor from John on the island of Patmos

Who? John, Jesus, the antichrist, the devil, seven churches in Asia Minor (Ephesus, Smyrna, Pergamum, Thyatira, Sardis, Philadelphia, Laodicea)

What? Via a series of beautiful and terrible glimpses into world events (and even into heaven itself), John attempts to describe the judgments of God, Christ's salvation of his church, and the coming new heaven and new earth. Though conflicting interpretations of the book's visions and symbols abound, one conclusion is unanimous: Revelation shows that in the ultimate battle between good and evil, God wins; in fact, he already has.

Really? The final word in Revelation and in the Bible is "Amen" (Revelation 22:21).

Why? Read Revelation for an unforgettable look at eternity.

Famous Verse: "'Yes, I am coming soon.' 'Amen. Come, Lord Jesus." —Revelation 22:20

GETTING TO THE HEART OF THE BIBLE: JESUS' LIFE AND TEACHINGS

Exhibit Hall 5
Exploring
the Content:
A Breakdown
of Bible Books

Exhibit Hall 7
Connecting
the Dots:
Jesus throughout
the Bible

Exhibit Hall 4
Meeting the
Characters:
A Who's Who
of Bible People

Exhibit Hall 8
Peeking into
the Future:
Heaven, Hell, and
Eternity

You are here.

Exhibit Hall 6
Getting to the
Heart of the Bible:
Jesus' Life and Teachings

Exhibit Hall 3
Grasping the Story:
A Time Line
of Bible History

Exhibit Hall 9
Summarizing
the Message:
Major Themes
in the Bible

Exhibit Hall 2
Getting Your
Bearings:
Basic Bible Geography

Exhibit Hall 1
Diving In:
A Quick Overview
of the Bible

Christians talk an awful lot about Jesus. But that's only because the Bible talks an awful lot about Jesus. His life and teachings are at the heart of the Bible and thus at the center of this *Self-Guided Tour of the Bible*.

Let's briefly review his incomparable life, remembering that we are only scratching the surface. As the apostle John said at the end of his Gospel: "Jesus did many other things as well. If every one of them were written down, I suppose that even the whole world would not have room for the books that would be written" (John 21:25).

Jesus is born.

"Today in the town of David a Savior has been born to you; he is the Messiah, the Lord." —Luke 2:11

Of the four Gospels, only Matthew and Luke provide accounts about the infancy of Christ. Both of these Gospels tell us that Jesus was miraculously conceived through the Holy Spirit and born to a virgin named Mary. This fulfilled an Old Testament prophecy that the Messiah would be born of a virgin and would be called *Immanuel*, which means "God with us" (Isaiah 7:14). Jesus' birth in Bethlehem (the "town of David") also fulfilled a prophecy made centuries earlier that the Messiah would be born in that small town (Micah 5:2; Matthew 2:1–6).

Luke paints for us the beautiful picture of Jesus' birth with details such as the manger Jesus sleeps in, the shepherds watching their flocks and rushing to see the newborn Savior, and the angels praising God.

Matthew focuses on the visit of the Magi (or wise men) who arrive to worship the newborn "king of the Jews" several days, weeks, or possibly even months after Jesus' birth, when Jesus and his parents are living in a "house" (Matthew 2:2, 11).

Read about this in Matthew 1:18–2:23; Luke 1:26–2:39.

Jesus grows up.

"And the child grew and became strong; he was filled with wisdom, and the grace of God was on him." —Luke 2:40

We know only one story from Jesus' childhood—the incident of him at age twelve being accidentally left behind in Jerusalem. His parents find him three days later at the temple in Jerusalem, astounding the religious leaders with his deep questions and insight. Other than this childhood incident, Luke says only that Jesus grew strong and tall in wisdom and in favor with God and people.

Since Jesus is called "the carpenter," he must have spent his youth and young adulthood learning this trade from and working with his earthly father Joseph (Mark 6:3).

Read about this in Luke 2:40–52.

Jesus gets baptized.

"Jesus came from Nazareth in Galilee and was baptized by John in the Jordan." —Mark 1:9

All four Gospels record Jesus being baptized at the age of thirty by John the Baptist. When Jesus comes out of the water of the Jordan River, God's Spirit descends on him like a dove and the Father in heaven declares, "This is my Son, whom I love; with him I am well pleased" (Matthew 3:17).

Read about this in Matthew 3:13–17; Mark 1:9–11; Luke 3:21–22; John 1:32–34.

Exhibit Hall 6

Jesus faces temptation.

"At once the Spirit sent him out into the wilderness, and he was in the wilderness forty days, being tempted by Satan."
—Mark 1:12–13

Matthew, Mark, and Luke record Jesus being led by the Holy Spirit into the wilderness for forty days of fasting and temptation by the devil. Jesus counters each satanic suggestion by quoting the truth of God's Word.

When the devil finally leaves him, angels minister to Jesus.

Read about this in Matthew 4:1–11; Mark 1:12–13; Luke 4:1–13.

Jesus preaches.

"'The time has come,' [Jesus] said. 'The kingdom of God has come near. Repent and believe the good news!'" —Mark 1:15

As Jesus begins proclaiming the arrival of the kingdom of God, he calls on people to do two things:

- *repent* (think and live differently); and
- *believe* the good news he is preaching.

This is the essence of the Christian faith.

Read about this in Matthew 4:17; Mark 1:14–15; Luke 4:14–15.

Jesus chooses disciples.

"'Come, follow me,' Jesus said, 'and I will send you out to fish for people.' At once they left their nets and followed him."
—Matthew 4:19–20

Jesus further calls those who believe his message to *follow*—that is, to become his disciples or students.

Central to Christ's ministry (and its long-term success) is the training of a group of twelve ordinary young men:

- Simon (also called Peter)
- Andrew (Peter's brother)
- James and John (Zebedee's sons) (these first four are fishermen by trade)
- Philip
- Bartholomew (also called Nathanael)
- Thomas
- Matthew (a tax collector)
- James (Alphaeus's son)
- Thaddaeus
- Simon (a Zealot)
- Judas Iscariot (who later betrays Jesus)

For three years, Jesus lives alongside them, gives them special training and assignments, and prepares them to take over his work after he returns to heaven.

Read about this in Matthew 4:18–22; 10:2–4; Mark 1:16–20; John 1:35–50.

Baptism

Christians have a lot of different ideas and beliefs about baptism, but most agree on the following truths about baptism:

- It's a command—not an option—for every follower of Jesus (Matthew 28:18–20).
- It's a meaningless ritual apart from faith.
- It's a way of publicly identifying with a teaching, person, or group.

Jesus' baptism was his way of identifying with John's message (the calling of sinful people to repent) and with the sinful people for whom he would die.

Exhibit Hall 6

Jesus performs miracles.

"Jesus went through all the towns and villages . . . healing every disease and sickness." —Matthew 9:35

There are more than forty miracles of Christ in the Gospels, including settings where we're told he "healed many" (Mark 1:34). In the Gospel of John, these supernatural acts are often called "signs"; they do exactly what a sign does—they point. They aren't meant to call attention to themselves but rather to point to something bigger and better. Whether demonstrating power over nature, demonic spirits, disease, or death, all of Jesus' miracles, or signs, point to his claims to be God in the flesh and the Savior of the world.

Read about this in Matthew 8:16; 9:35; Mark 3:10; 4:35–41; Luke 7:11–17; John 11:1–44.

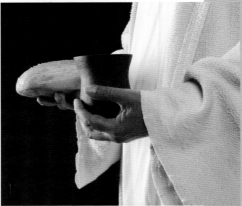

Jesus challenges the status quo.

"Woe to you, teachers of the law and Pharisees, you hypocrites! You shut the door of the kingdom of heaven in people's faces." —Matthew 23:13

Time and again during his three-year ministry, Jesus confronts the prevailing religious system. At times his critiques of first-century Judaism's empty ritualism are mere verbal barbs. On other occasions, there are heated discussions. The callous and hypocritical actions of some scribes and Pharisees anger Jesus. He sternly pronounces "woes" on these leaders, calling them hypocrites, fools,

and blind guides. He even enters the part of the temple they've turned into a moneymaking market, overturns their tables, and drives them out! We see the leaders' curiosity turn to concern and then morph into a calculated plan to kill Jesus.

Read about this in Matthew 6:1–5; 23:13–39; Mark 3:1–5; 11:15–18.

Jesus teaches God's truth.

"The people were amazed at his teaching, because he taught them as one who had authority." —Mark 1:22

Most of Jesus' disciple-making ministry involved teaching and training—and Jesus was a master teacher!

Let's look quickly at *how* and *what* Jesus taught.

How did Jesus teach?

- **He taught in varied settings.** He addressed big crowds—sometimes in the thousands (Matthew 7:28; 13:2; Mark 4:1). He often taught his smaller group of twelve (John 14–17) and also addressed individuals one-on-one (John 3–4).

- **He taught with authority**, meaning his words were weighty, piercing, and not easily dismissed (Mark 1:22).

- **He taught with creativity.** He seized on teachable moments in order to explain important truths to people (Luke 7:18–29, 36–50).

- **He taught by asking questions.** Look, for example, at Mark 8: "How many loaves do you have?" (verse 5); "Why does this generation ask for a sign?" (verse 12); "Do you still not see or understand?" (verse 17); "Do you see anything?" (verse 23); "Who do people say I am?" (verse 27).

- **He taught by lecture**, much like a modern-day preacher might do (Matthew 5–7; Luke 6:20–49).

- **He taught by telling parables.** In a nutshell, a parable takes simple, everyday situations (a lost coin, a weed-infested wheat field, a man about to lose his job, etc.) and uses them to convey a larger spiritual truth. About 35 percent of all that Jesus taught is contained in these ingenious little stories.

The Parables of Jesus

Jesus often taught in parables, so those with open hearts could understand (Matthew 13:11–15). Here are thirty-seven parables of Jesus with quick summaries and Scripture references for each.

	Parable	Lesson	Reference
1	Bags of Money	God expects us to faithfully use the things he gives us.	Matthew 25:14–30
2	Barren Fig Tree	God doesn't give us endless chances.	Luke 13:6–9
3	Building a Tower and Going to War	Consider the cost before making commitments.	Luke 14:28–33
4	Dragnet	A fishing net catches everything in its path, but only the good fish (the people made righteous by Jesus) are kept.	Matthew 13:47–50
5	Good Samaritan	Help others regardless of the risk or situation.	Luke 10:30–37
6	Great Banquet	Put Jesus first.	Luke 14:16–24
7	Growing Seed	We plant God's seed and wait for it to grow.	Mark 4:26–29
8	Hidden Treasure	When we discover God's great treasure, we pursue it at all costs.	Matthew 13:44
9	Hired Hands	Regardless of how long we serve Jesus, we all have the same reward.	Matthew 20:1–16
10	House on the Rock	Wise people build their lives on the stable foundation of God's truth.	Luke 6:47–49
11	Faithful and Wise Manager	Serve God faithfully at all times and in all situations.	Luke 12:42–48
12	Fig Tree	Look for signs of the kingdom of God.	Matthew 24:32–34
13	Friend in Need	God will give us what we need if we ask him.	Luke 11:5–13
14	Lamp on a Stand	Let your light shine; don't hide it.	Luke 8:16–17; 11:33–36
15	Lazy Servants	God wants us to serve others and not expect people to wait on us.	Luke 17:7–10
16	Lost Coin	Rejoicing breaks out in heaven each time someone decides to follow Jesus.	Luke 15:8–10
17	Lost Sheep	God seeks us just as a shepherd looks for his one wayward sheep.	Matthew 18:12–14

Exhibit Hall 6

	Parable	Lesson	Reference
18	Mustard Seed	A tiny bit of faith can produce huge results.	Luke 13:18–19
19	New Cloth on an Old Garment	Some things don't mix, such as the teachings of Jesus and the religious teachers of his day.	Luke 5:36
20	New Wine in Old Wineskins	We can't add the gospel of Jesus to old religious systems and ways.	Luke 5:37–38
21	Persistent Widow	God answers our prayers.	Luke 18:1–8
22	Pharisee and Tax Collector	God appreciates humility and despises pride.	Luke 18:9–14
23	Prodigal Son	God desires for us to return to him.	Luke 15:11–32
24	Rich Fool	We need to trust God, not wealth, to save us.	Luke 12:16–21
25	Rich Man and Lazarus	Our eternal reward may not match our earthly status.	Luke 16:19–31
26	Shrewd Manager	Will we serve God or money?	Luke 16:1–13
27	Sower	We must tell everyone about Jesus, but not everyone will receive him.	Luke 8:4–15
28	Two Sons	What we do matters more than what we say.	Matthew 21:28–32
29	Two Debtors	The greater our sin, the more we appreciate God's forgiveness.	Luke 7:41–43
30	Unforgiving Servant	God forgives us completely; we must do the same for others.	Matthew 18:23–35
31	Valuable Pearl	When we find God's priceless pearl (Jesus), we should willingly give up everything else to follow him.	Matthew 13:45–46
32	Watchful Servants	Be ready for Jesus to return at any time.	Luke 12:35–40
33	Wedding Feast	Jesus invites all, but not everyone accepts his offer.	Matthew 22:2–14
34	Weeds	We must wait until the end, at harvest time, for God to remove the evil in our world.	Matthew 13:24–30
35	Wicked Renters	God punishes disobedience.	Matthew 21:33–45
36	Wise and Foolish Bridesmaids	Christ will return without warning.	Matthew 25:1–13
37	Yeast	A small amount of God's kingdom transforms everything it touches.	Luke 13:20–21

What did Jesus teach?

It might be simpler to ask about the topics Jesus *didn't* teach on. Much of his discussing and debating and sparring with the Jewish religious leaders revolved around matters of the Law of Moses (Matthew 12; 16:1–12; 21:23–27; Mark 11:27–12:34; Luke 11:37–54).

Here are some other prominent themes we see in Jesus' teaching.

- **The Reality of the Kingdom of God (Kingdom of Heaven)**

  Matthew 3:2; 4:17; 5–7; 13; Mark 4; Luke 17:20–21

  "Repent, for the kingdom of heaven has come near." —Matthew 3:2

- **The Importance of Faith**

  Matthew 6:25–34; 8:10; Mark 11:22–23; Luke 7:9; 8:25; 17:5–6; 22:32

  "If you have faith as small as a mustard seed, you can say to this mountain, 'Move from here to there,' and it will move. Nothing will be impossible for you." —Matthew 17:20

THE KINGDOM OF GOD

The phrase "kingdom of God" occurs close to seventy times in the Bible, all in the New Testament. As an alternative, the phrase "kingdom of heaven," which occurs in his Gospel just over thirty times, is usually used by Matthew. This gives us about one hundred New Testament references to the coming spiritual kingdom through Jesus. Jesus compared this kingdom, this rule of God, to all kinds of things: a mustard seed, yeast, a treasure in a field, a pearl of great worth, a fishing expedition (Matthew 13). And he said the important thing is to seek God's kingdom first (Matthew 6:33) and to devote our lives to becoming human answers to the following prayer: "Your kingdom come" (Matthew 6:10).

- **The High Cost of Following Jesus**

  Matthew 10:24–39; 16:24–27; Mark 8:31–38; Luke 9:23–25, 57–62; 14:25–35

  "Whoever wants to be my disciple must deny themselves and take up their cross and follow me." —Mark 8:34

- **God's Love for Sinners**

  Matthew 23:37; Luke 15; John 3:16–21

  "For God so loved the world that he gave his one and only Son, that whoever believes in him shall not perish but have eternal life." —John 3:16

- **How to Have Eternal Life**

  John 3:16; 5:24; 6:40, 47; 10:28; 14:6; 17:3

  "Whoever hears my word and believes him who sent me has eternal life." —John 5:24

- **The Importance of the Heart**

  Matthew 12:33–37; 13:10–17; Mark 7; Luke 16:14–15

  "You are the ones who justify yourselves in the eyes of others, but God knows your hearts." —Luke 16:15

- **The Priority of Love**

  Matthew 5:43–48; 22:34–40; Mark 12:28–31; Luke 6:27–36; John 13:34–35; 15:12–17

  "One of them, an expert in the law, tested him with this question: 'Teacher, which is the greatest commandment in the Law?' Jesus replied: 'Love the Lord your God with all your heart and with all your soul and with all your mind. This is the first and greatest commandment. And the second is like it: Love your neighbor as yourself.'" —Matthew 22:35–39

- **Prayer**

  Matthew 6:5–13; 7:7–11; 18:19–20; 26:36–46; Luke 11:1–13; 18:1–8; 21:36; 22:39–46; John 17

  "This, then, is how you should pray: Our Father in heaven, hallowed be your name, your kingdom come, your will be done, on earth as it is in heaven. Give us today our daily bread. And forgive us our debts, as we also have forgiven our debtors. And lead us not into temptation, but deliver us from the evil one." —Matthew 6:9–13

Relationships

Matthew 5:21–26; 7:12; 12:46–50; 18:15–17

"So in everything, do to others what you would have them do to you." —Matthew 7:12

Marriage and Divorce

Matthew 5:27–32; 19:1–12; Mark 10:1–12; Luke 16:18

"For this reason a man will leave his father and mother and be united to his wife, and the two will become one flesh.' So they are no longer two, but one flesh. Therefore what God has joined together, let no one separate." —Mark 10:7–9

The Necessity of Forgiveness

Matthew 5:38–42; 6:12–15; 18:21–35; Mark 11:25; Luke 17:3–4

"If you hold anything against anyone, forgive them, so that your Father in heaven may forgive you your sins." —Mark 11:25

The Danger of Money

Matthew 6:19–24; 17:24–27; 19:16–26; Mark 10:17–27; 12:41–44; Luke 12:13–34; 21:1–4

"No one can serve two masters. . . . You cannot serve both God and money." —Matthew 6:24

The Priority (and Reward) of Serving Others

Matthew 10:5–42; 19:27–30; 20:20–28; 25:14–30; Mark 10:28–45; Luke 9:6; 16:1–13; 18:28–30; John 13:1–17

"Whoever wants to become great among you must be your servant, and whoever wants to be first must be slave of all." —Mark 10:43–44

Jesus teaching his disciples how to pray

- ### The Reality of Heaven and Hell

  Matthew 7:13–14; 18:12–14; 20:1–16; Luke 13:22–30; 16:19–31; John 14:1–6

  "My Father's house has many rooms. . . . And if I go and prepare a place for you, I will come back and take you to be with me that you also may be where I am." —John 14:2–3

- ### Hypocrisy and Pride

  Matthew 6:1–4, 16–18; 7:15–23; 15:1–14; Mark 7:1–23; Luke 7:36–50; 18:9–14

  "For all those who exalt themselves will be humbled, and those who humble themselves will be exalted." —Luke 18:14

- ### The Inevitability of Persecution and Suffering

  Matthew 5:11, 44; 10:16–23; Mark 6:7–13; John 15:18–21

  "Blessed are you when people insult you, persecute you and falsely say all kinds of evil against you because of me." —Matthew 5:11

Jesus and the rich, young ruler (Matthew 19:16–26)

- ### The Holy Spirit

  John 14:16–26; 16:5–15; 20:22

  "The Holy Spirit . . . will teach you all things and will remind you of everything I have said to you." —John 14:26

- ### The Future

  Matthew 16:27; 24–25; Mark 13; Luke 12:35–48; 21:5–36

  "Therefore keep watch, because you do not know on what day your Lord will come." —Matthew 24:42

THE END TIMES

Without giving details about *when*, Jesus talked a lot about the last days of earth. In brief, he said:

- There will be false prophets and false disciples (Matthew 7:15–23).

- Many will be deceived (Matthew 24:11, 24; Mark 13:22; Luke 21:8).

- There will be "wars and rumors of wars," natural disasters, pestilences around the world, "and fearful events and great signs from heaven" (Matthew 24:6–8; Luke 21:10–11).

- Lawlessness will increase and cause people to be spiritually indifferent (Matthew 24:12).

- Believers will face persecution because of their faith in Jesus (Luke 21:12–19).

- Armies will surround Jerusalem (Luke 21:20).

- "The abomination that causes desolation" will stand in the holy place (Matthew 24:15–21). This mysterious event was first revealed by the prophet Daniel, and though Bible scholars can only speculate about what this "abomination" refers to, it will likely be self-evident at the time it occurs (Daniel 9:27).

- Christ will come a second time to earth, in a flash, just as lightning streaks across the sky (Matthew 24:27). He will come "in a cloud with power and great glory" (Luke 21:27).

- A time of judgment will follow Christ's return (Matthew 24:42–51; 25:31–46).

Jesus weeps over Jerusalem (Luke 19:41–44)

Jesus experiences a tumultuous final week.

"For even the Son of Man [Jesus] did not come to be served, but to serve, and to give his life as a ransom for many." —Mark 10:45

So many important things happened during Jesus' final week leading up to—and including—his death and resurrection that the Gospel writers focus an inordinate amount of attention there. For Matthew this amounts to eight of his twenty-eight chapters. Mark devotes six of his sixteen chapters to events during Jesus' final week, and Luke dedicates five and a half of his twenty-four chapters to these eventful days. Ten of John's twenty-one chapters zero in on Christ's final days—plus the days immediately following his crucifixion and resurrection.

Let's look briefly at what transpired.

JESUS' FINAL WEEK

SUNDAY	Jesus enters Jerusalem riding on a donkey.
MONDAY	Jesus weeps over Jerusalem. He also drives out the merchants from the temple.
TUESDAY	Jesus teaches in the temple and on the Mount of Olives.
WEDNESDAY	Judas conspires (possibly on this day) with the religious leaders to arrest Jesus.
THURSDAY	Jesus shares a meal (the Last Supper) with his disciples and then prays alone in the Garden of Gethsemane. He is betrayed by Judas, arrested, and sent to stand trial.
FRIDAY	Jesus is sentenced, beaten, and crucified. After his death on the cross, Jesus' body is buried in a tomb.
SATURDAY	This day is the Sabbath, the day of rest.
SUNDAY	Jesus' followers discover that Jesus has risen from the dead. He appears to his disciples and many others.

Exhibit Hall 6

Jesus enters Jerusalem.

Jesus rides into Jerusalem on a donkey and is hailed by the masses as they lay palm branches along his path. This fulfilled the prophecy in Zechariah 9:9: "See, your king comes to you, righteous and victorious, lowly and riding on a donkey." (This event is known as the Triumphal Entry and the day is now celebrated as Palm Sunday.)

Read about this in Matthew 21:1–11; Mark 11:1–11; Luke 19:28–44; John 12:12–19.

Jesus clears out the temple.

Jesus weeps over the city of Jerusalem because its people do not recognize him as their Messiah and would soon reject him. He also clears out the temple in Jerusalem, driving away the money changers and those who were selling animals.

Read about this in Matthew 21:12–17; Mark 11:12–19; Luke 19:45–46.

Jesus teaches.

Jesus teaches in the temple and speaks ominous words about the future from the Mount of Olives just outside Jerusalem.

Read about this in Matthew 21:18–26:2; Mark 11:20–13:37; Luke 19:47–21:38; John 12:20–50.

Judas and the leaders plot.

The chief priests and elders give Judas Iscariot—one of Jesus' twelve disciples—thirty pieces of silver to arrange a way to have Jesus secretly arrested.

Read about this in Matthew 26:3–16; Mark 14:1–11; Luke 22:1–6.

Jesus and his disciples share a last meal.

Jesus and his disciples gather in a rented upstairs room in Jerusalem to eat the Passover meal. He washes their feet (a customary task normally performed by servants) in order to model for them an attitude of humility and selflessness. He also teaches them some important final lessons and establishes the practice and significance of Communion (the Lord's Supper).

Read about this in Matthew 26:17–35; Mark 14:12–31; Luke 22:7–38; John 13:1–17:26

Jesus prays.

After the meal, as he anticipates the gruesome death he knows is coming, Jesus goes to the Garden of Gethsemane to pray fervently for his Father's will to be done.

Read about this in Matthew 26:36–46; Mark 14:32–42; Luke 22:39–46; John 18:1.

Jesus is arrested.

In the late night hours, as Jesus finishes praying in Gethsemane, Judas Iscariot (one of Jesus' disciples) arrives with a detachment of soldiers and some of the Jewish religious leaders. He gives the signal, betraying Jesus with a kiss. Peter draws his sword and slashes off the ear of a man named Malchus. Jesus tells his bold, impulsive disciple to stand down, and then he heals the man's ear. The mob arrests Jesus and leads him away.

Read about this in Matthew 26:47–56; Mark 14:43–52; Luke 22:47–53; John 18:2–11.

Exhibit Hall 6

Jesus is tried, denied, and crucified.

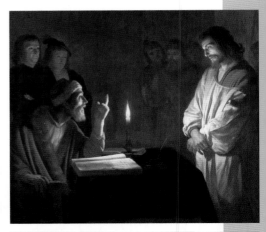

Jesus' arrest begins a long night of illegal trials.

The high priest, the chief priests, and elders and teachers of the law—who normally don't agree on much of anything—unite wholeheartedly in their opposition to Jesus. Even though the witnesses testifying against Jesus give inconsistent and conflicting testimony, the leaders decide Jesus is guilty of blasphemy and deserves to die.

Meanwhile, Peter faces his own ordeal. Despite his earlier pledge of absolute commitment to the Lord (even expressing a willingness to die for him), Peter denies three times having any involvement with Jesus or even knowing him.

Since the religious leaders lack legal authority to carry out an execution, they seek approval from the Roman government. The Roman governor of that region, Pontius Pilate, rejects their case for executing Jesus. When they persist, Pilate sends Jesus to King Herod Antipas. Herod welcomes the opportunity to interview Jesus—and maybe see a miracle. When Jesus won't answer questions, Herod and his soldiers mock Jesus and send him back to Pilate. Pilate wants to free Jesus, but when a mob forms and threatens to riot, the Roman governor reluctantly sentences Christ to death.

The soldiers take Jesus away, strip him, mock him, beat and flog him. When they grow weary of ridiculing him, they crucify him between two common criminals. Some six gruesome hours later, Jesus is dead.

Read about this in Matthew 26:57–27:56; Mark 14:53–15:41; Luke 22:54–23:49; John 18:12–19:37.

Exhibit Hall 6

Jesus is buried.

After Jesus dies, a godly man from Arimathea named Joseph (a member of the Jewish council who had opposed the plan to kill Jesus) goes to Pilate to request Jesus' body. When Pilate agrees, Joseph hastily wraps Jesus' body and places it in a new tomb just before sundown on Friday when the Sabbath begins. He covers the opening of the tomb with a large stone. This fulfills Isaiah's prophecy that the Messiah's body will lie in a rich man's tomb (Isaiah 53:9). Pilate ensures that the tomb entrance is sealed and guarded by Roman soldiers.

Read about this in Matthew 27:57–66; Mark 15:42–47; Luke 23:50–56; John 19:38–42.

Jesus rises from the dead.

"The angel said to the women, 'Do not be afraid, for I know that you are looking for Jesus, who was crucified. He is not here; he has risen, just as he said.'" —Matthew 28:5–6

Early Sunday morning, some female followers of Jesus go to his tomb. Their plan is to complete the burial preparations of Jesus' body that Joseph was unable to perform because of the start of the Sabbath. They find the stone removed and Jesus' body gone. Angels confirm that Jesus has risen—just as he had said. The women go and tell all this to the disciples.

Over the next weeks, Jesus appears to the eleven disciples (Judas Iscariot had taken his own life after betraying Jesus). Many of them witnessed the resurrected Jesus multiple times. Even "Doubting Thomas" sees and believes. Another of Jesus' resurrection appearances happens by the Sea of Galilee, where Jesus makes a special point to restore Peter after his heartbreaking denial of his Lord.

Read about this in Matthew 28:1–15; Mark 16:1–8; Luke 24:1–49; John 20:1–21:25.

Jesus returns to heaven.

**"While he was blessing them, he left them and was taken up into heaven."
—Luke 24:51**

In his final act on earth as the resurrected, victorious Savior, Jesus tells his disciples to wait together in Jerusalem until God gives them the Spirit's power.

Then they are to take the good news everywhere and make disciples of all people. This is crucial because Jesus is coming again.

Read about this in Matthew 28:16–20; Luke 24:50–53; Acts 1:3–11.

**"After [Jesus] said this, he was taken up before their very eyes, and a cloud hid him from their sight. . . . When suddenly two men dressed in white stood beside them. 'Men of Galilee,' they said, 'why do you stand here looking into the sky? This same Jesus, who has been taken from you into heaven, will come back in the same way you have seen him go into heaven.'
—Acts 1:11**

One Very Important Question

That's a very concise summary of what Matthew, Mark, Luke, and John reveal about the life and teachings of Jesus. And all those incidents, teachings, miracles, and misunderstandings raise a very important question. It's a question Jesus himself once asked his followers as they were traveling in Caesarea Philippi.

> On the way he asked them, "Who do people say I am?"
>
> They replied, "Some say John the Baptist; others say Elijah; and still others, one of the prophets."
>
> "But what about you?" he asked. "Who do you say I am?"
>
> —Mark 8:27–29

There it is: "Who do you say I am?" This is the question above all other questions. This is the most significant question anyone can ever wrestle with in this fleeting life.

C. S. Lewis was right when he argued that the claims of Jesus are either of *no importance* (if they are false) or of *utmost importance* (if they are true). The one thing they cannot be, he concluded, is of *moderate importance.*

To the question of Jesus' identity, it's possible to answer as many people did in Jesus' day: "Jesus was a great moral teacher and prophet." Or you can answer like so many do today: "He was a good man, a political revolutionary, a mystic, a miracle worker, a misunderstood martyr."

Or you can look at all that Jesus said and did and conclude with Peter: "You are the Messiah" (Mark 8:29).

JESUS' CLAIMS ABOUT HIMSELF

In the Gospel of John, we find numerous claims by Jesus as to his true identity:

» **I am** . . . he (the Messiah) (John 4:26; 8:24; 13:19; 18:5, 8).

» **I am** . . . the bread of life (John 6:35, 41, 48, 51).

» **I am** . . . from God (John 7:29).

» **I am** . . . the light of the world (John 8:12; 9:5).

» **I am** . . . from above (John 8:23).

» **I am** . . . the Son of Man (John 8:28).

» **I am** . . . I AM (the name by which God revealed himself to Moses in Exodus 3:14; John 8:58).

» **I am** . . . the gate/door (John 10:7, 9).

» **I am** . . . the good shepherd (John 10:11, 14).

» **I am** . . . the Son of God (John 10:36).

» **I am** . . . the resurrection and the life (John 11:25).

» **I am** . . . Teacher and Lord (John 13:13).

» **I am** . . . the way and the truth and the life (John 14:6).

» **I am** . . . in the Father (John 14:10–11, 20).

» **I am** . . . the true vine (John 15:1, 5).

» **I am** . . . not of the world (John 17:14, 16).

» **I am** . . . a king (John 18:37).

"I am the way and the truth and the life. No one comes to the Father except through me." —John 14:6

Jesus shows us the *way* to God and provides us with the *truth* about God. What's more, Jesus offers us the *life* that only God can give—new life, eternal life, a rich and satisfying life.

It's important to note that Jesus claims unapologetically that he is *the* way, *the* truth, and *the* life—not *a* way or *one of many* truths. In case anyone might miss that critical distinction, Jesus adds, "No one comes to the Father except through me" (John 14:6).

People often dismiss Jesus' claims or argue about why there aren't ten or a hundred or a million ways to God. But knowing there's a way to have a relationship with God through Jesus gives us a reason not to argue but to celebrate! Jesus says if we know him, we know the Father. If we see Jesus, we see the Father (John 14:7).

The more you study and reflect on the story of Jesus' life, death, and resurrection, the more you'll understand why it is called the *gospel*. *Gospel* means "good news."

Hopefully this minicourse on Jesus serves only to whet your appetite. A wise person will put this little book down and open the Gospels. May that person be you. May *you* marvel at the One who is at the heart of the Bible.

Exhibit Hall 6

CONNECTING THE DOTS:
JESUS THROUGHOUT THE BIBLE

Exhibit Hall 5
Exploring the
Content:
A Breakdown
of Bible Books

Exhibit Hall 7
Connecting
the Dots:
Jesus throughout
the Bible
You are here.

Exhibit Hall 4
Meeting the
Characters:
A Who's Who
of Bible People

Exhibit Hall 8
Peeking into
the Future:
Heaven, Hell, and
Eternity

Exhibit Hall 6
Getting to the Heart
of the Bible:
Jesus' Life and Teachings

Exhibit Hall 3
Grasping the Story:
A Time Line
of Bible History

Exhibit Hall 9
Summarizing
the Message:
Major Themes
in the Bible

Exhibit Hall 2
Getting Your
Bearings:
Basic Bible Geography

Exhibit Hall 1
Diving In:
A Quick Overview
of the Bible

Some people might read the Old and New Testaments and come away with the idea that the Bible is two disconnected parts. But the entire Bible is one story with one plot and one main character. Here's a truth that can help us connect all the dots and clear up some of the mystery of the Bible: *From beginning to end, the Bible is about Jesus.*

It's true. In Scripture, everything points to Jesus. The Old Testament—with all those laws—*anticipates* his coming. Then, after the Gospels (Matthew, Mark, Luke, and John) describe his life, death, resurrection, and return to heaven, Acts and all of the epistles in the New Testament *look back* on his coming. The final book of the Bible *looks ahead* to his second coming. The Bible is about Jesus. And the point of the Bible isn't for us to follow a long list of laws or *try* really hard to be something; it's for us to *trust* Jesus!

This wouldn't be much of a guidebook if we ignored this monumental truth. So we've devoted a whole section to showing how Jesus is the heart of the Bible—how he peeks out from just about every page.

WHAT IS TYPOLOGY?

Biblically speaking, *typology* is the study of how certain people, objects, or events in the Old Testament foreshadow or hint at a coming person, object, or event in the New Testament.

For example, the incident in the Old Testament when the rebellious Israelites were punished by an outbreak of poisonous snakes is a *type*. Moses made a bronze serpent and lifted it up on a pole. All who looked at it were healed (Numbers 21:4–9). Later in the New Testament, Jesus said this event of the bronze serpent pointed forward to his own death on the cross. He would be lifted up. And all those who looked to him (i.e., trusted in him) would be saved (John 3:14–15).

When we read the Old Testament, we find numerous *types* like that. In other words, the Old Testament continuously points to Jesus!

While we can't list every allusion and reference to Jesus in the Old Testament, here are twenty of the biggies.

Jesus is . . .

1. EVE'S OFFSPRING WHO CRUSHES SATAN

"The reason the Son of God appeared was to destroy the devil's work." —1 John 3:8

The Reference

In Genesis 3, after Adam and Eve listen to the serpent (Satan) and disobey God, God spells out the consequences of their action, including an ongoing hostility between the snake and Eve's descendants. Then God tells the serpent, "[Eve's offspring] will crush your head, and you will strike his heel" (Genesis 3:15).

The Realization

When Jesus was dying on the cross, it may have looked like he had lost—as if Satan had struck at Jesus and won. But three days later when Jesus rose from the dead, he proved that he had crushed Satan. Though Jesus suffered short-term torment for us, he permanently defeated the evil one at the cross.

2. THE LAST ADAM

"For as in Adam all die, so in Christ all will be made alive." —1 Corinthians 15:22

The Reference

In the Old Testament, we meet Adam, the first man, who chooses to disobey God, which plunges the world into sin and death (Genesis 1–4).

The Realization

In the New Testament, the apostle Paul speaks of Jesus as "the last Adam," who is able to make all alive (1 Corinthians 15:45). Jesus reversed the curse of sin and death (Romans 5:12–17).

3. OUR HIGH PRIEST AND KING

"He will be clothed with majesty and will sit and rule on his throne. And he will be a priest on his throne." —Zechariah 6:13

The Reference

After victory in battle, Abraham meets a man named Melchizedek, described as the king of Salem and a priest of God. Melchizedek blesses Abraham. Abraham gives this strange king a tenth of the spoils (Genesis 14:17–20). Melchizedek is unique: No one else in the Old Testament serves as both king and priest.

The Old Testament prophet Zechariah foretells that Israel's Messiah will be both king and priest, bringing harmony between the monarchy and the priesthood (Zechariah 6:12–13).

The Realization

The book of Hebrews in the New Testament tells us that Melchizedek foreshadowed Jesus, the ultimate King and High Priest. When the writer of Hebrews says that Melchizedek was "without beginning of days or end of life," we think of Christ (Hebrews 7:3).

THE TORN VEIL

Once a year Israel's high priest would go into a secluded temple room called the Most Holy Place. Behind a thick veil that separated this holy room from the rest of the temple, the high priest would offer a solemn sacrifice to God for the sins of Israel.

At the moment Jesus died on the cross, this veil in the temple miraculously "was torn in two from top to bottom" (Matthew 27:51). This signified that Jesus' death on the cross had opened the way of access to God—not just for priests, but for everyone!

Jesus was, and is, our perfect High Priest who makes a way for everyone who trusts in him to enter into God's presence.

4. OUR SUBSTITUTE SACRIFICE

"[Jesus] himself bore our sins in his body on the cross, so that we might die to sins and live for righteousness." —1 Peter 2:24

The Reference

In Genesis 22, God tells Abraham to sacrifice his beloved son Isaac as an offering. With young Isaac bound and lying on the altar, God intervenes at the last second. He calls Abraham's attention to a ram that is in a nearby thicket. This ram stands in for Isaac and dies in his place.

The Realization

Abraham's willingness to sacrifice his son foreshadowed God's sacrifice of his own Son. The ram, which God graciously provided, is a *type* of Jesus, who would stand in as our substitute sacrifice (Luke 22:19–20).

5. OUR PASSOVER LAMB

"The next day John saw Jesus coming toward him and said, 'Look, the Lamb of God, who takes away the sin of the world!'" —John 1:29

The Reference

In Exodus 7–12, God sends a series of devastating judgments on Egypt to convince hard-hearted Pharaoh to release the Israelites from slavery. The tenth and final plague is death to the firstborn male of each household, *unless* the blood of a lamb without defect is sprinkled over the house's doorway. God promises to "pass over" these homes, so the plague of death will not touch their households (Exodus 12:13).

The Realization

The New Testament says that Christ is our Passover lamb—the Lamb of God who takes away our sins and saves us from eternal death (John 1:36; Romans 5:10; 1 Corinthians 5:7).

6. THE ROCK

The ancient Israelites "drank from the spiritual rock that accompanied them, and that rock was Christ." —1 Corinthians 10:4

The Reference

In Exodus 17:1–7, the Israelites can't find water in the arid wilderness, so they blame Moses. God tells Moses to stand before the people at the rock at Horeb and strike the rock with his staff. When he does, water gushes forth, and the people are saved.

The Realization

The New Testament calls Jesus our rock (Romans 9:33; 1 Peter 2:8). He claimed to be the One from whom living water flows and who quenches our deepest thirsts (John 4:10–14; 7:38).

7. THE SCAPEGOAT

"You know that [Jesus] appeared so that he might take away our sins." —1 John 3:5

The Reference

In Leviticus 16, God tells the Israelites to conduct an annual ritual involving two goats. One goat is to be sacrificed as a sin offering for the people. In front of the people, the high priest is to lay his hands on the second goat and confess the people's sins, symbolically laying the sins on the goat's head. Then the goat, called the scapegoat, is taken far away and released in the wilderness.

The Realization

The scapegoat of the Old Testament foreshadowed Jesus as our ultimate scapegoat who takes away our sins forever (Hebrews 10:1–14).

8. A PROPHET LIKE MOSES

Moses said, "The Lord your God will raise up for you a prophet like me from among your own people." —Acts 3:22

The Reference

In Deuteronomy 18:15–19, Moses speaks of a future prophet who will be like himself.

The Realization

The New Testament declares that Jesus is that prophet (Acts 3:22–26).

Jesus is "like" Moses in that Jesus and Moses were both:

	Moses	Jesus
Threatened in infancy by a murderous ruler	Exodus 1:1–2:10	Matthew 2:1–20
Humble	Numbers 12:3	Matthew 11:29
Commissioned to lead captives to freedom	Exodus 3:10	Luke 4:17–21
A bold intercessor	Numbers 11:2	John 17:1–26
Mediator of a covenant	Exodus 19:5	Hebrews 9:15

9. THE CLOUD AND THE FIRE

Jesus said: "Whoever follows me will never walk in darkness, but will have the light of life." —John 8:12

The Reference

Passages like Exodus 13:21–22 and Numbers 14:14 describe how God led the Israelites via a massive cloud during the day and a pillar of fire at night as they roamed around the desert south of Canaan for forty years. The constant cloud and fire guided the people and reminded them of God's constant presence with them.

The Realization

The cloud and fire serve as a *type* of Jesus. He is our light and our guide who will never leave us (Matthew 28:20; John 12:46). We are to follow him (Mark 1:17).

10. THE BRONZE SERPENT

"Just as Moses lifted up the snake in the wilderness, so the Son of Man must be lifted up, that everyone who believes may have eternal life in him." —John 3:14–15

The Reference

In Numbers 21:4–9, when the people of God grumble and rebel against God, they are bitten by poisonous snakes. God instructs Moses to fashion a serpent out of bronze and hoist it up on a pole. Anyone with a snakebite will live if he or she simply looks at the bronze serpent lifted up on the pole.

The Realization

In John 3, Jesus says this bronze serpent refers to him being lifted up (on the cross). The consequence for our sin is death, but we will live if we look to him for our salvation (Romans 6:23).

11. OUR GUARDIAN-REDEEMER

"You know the grace of our Lord Jesus Christ, that though he was rich, yet for your sake he became poor, so that you through his poverty might become rich." —2 Corinthians 8:9

The Reference

In the book of Ruth, the upstanding Boaz buys property from his relative Naomi and marries her widowed daughter-in-law Ruth to continue their family line. In doing so, Boaz acts as "a guardian-redeemer" (Ruth 3:9), providing a future for Ruth and Naomi, rescuing them from poverty and the risk of starvation.

The Realization

In the New Testament, Jesus acts like Boaz. He rescues us from spiritual poverty and makes Christians (the church) his bride (Ephesians 5:25–33; Revelation 21:1–9; 22:17).

12. GOD'S ANOINTED ONE

"God anointed Jesus of Nazareth with the Holy Spirit and power; . . . he went around doing good and healing all who were under the power of the devil, because God was with him." —Acts 10:38

The Reference

In 1 Samuel 2:35, God tells Eli the priest that he will raise up "a faithful priest" who will act according to God's "heart and mind." God calls this priest his "anointed one." Other Old Testament passages echo this description (Psalm 132:10, 17; Daniel 9:25–26).

The Realization

In the New Testament, Jesus is repeatedly spoken of as God's anointed (Luke 4:18; Acts 10:38; Hebrews 1:9). He is the faithful priest who does everything God wills. The word *Messiah* (or *Christ* in Greek) comes from a Hebrew word that means "anointed one" (John 4:25–26).

13. DESCENDANT OF DAVID

God said to David: "Your house and your kingdom will endure forever before me; your throne will be established forever.'" —2 Samuel 7:16

The Reference

In 2 Samuel 7:12–16, God promises David that his royal line will last forever, extending throughout eternity. But when the Babylonians decimated the kingdom of Judah, King David's royal lineage came to an end—or did it?

The Realization

We learn in the New Testament that Jesus was a direct descendant of David (Matthew 1:1–17; Luke 3:23–38). But unlike the kings of centuries past, Jesus did not set up an earthly kingdom. Instead, he pointed us to the kingdom of God. Jesus is the ultimate King of Kings who will rule over all creation for eternity (Revelation 19:16). In this sense, David's kingly line lives on through Jesus, David's earthly descendant (Luke 1:27; 2 Timothy 2:8).

14. THE SUFFERING

"The virgin will conceive and give birth to a son, and they will call him *Immanuel* (which means 'God with us')." —Matthew 1:23 (Isaiah 7:14)

Hundreds of years before Jesus' birth, the prophet Isaiah gave details about Israel's coming Messiah. The New Testament shows how Jesus fulfilled all these prophecies.

The Reference	The Realization
Be born of a virgin (Isaiah 7:14).	Jesus was miraculously born of the Virgin Mary (Luke 1:34).
Heal the blind, lame, deaf, and mute (Isaiah 35:5–6).	Jesus healed many people during his time on earth (Matthew 4:23).
Be preceded by a forerunner (Isaiah 40:3).	John the Baptist prepared the way for Jesus' ministry (Mark 1:1–8).
Be despised by his own people (Isaiah 49:7).	Jesus was rejected by the religious leaders of his day and ultimately crucified (Matthew 12:14; 27:32–50; Luke 4:14–30).
Be humble in appearance (Isaiah 53:2).	Though fully God, Jesus humbled himself to become fully human (Philippians 2:6–8).
Give himself as an offering (Isaiah 53:10).	Jesus willingly went to the cross (John 10:18).
Bear the sins of many (Isaiah 53:12).	In his death, he bore the punishment for all humanity's sin (1 Peter 2:24).

15. THE BRANCH

"I will raise up for David a righteous Branch, a King who will reign wisely and do what is just and right in the land." —Jeremiah 23:5

The Reference

Three prophets—Isaiah, Jeremiah, and Zechariah—use the image of a branch, shoot, or root that sprouts from David's line, grows, spreads out, and reigns as a wise and good king (Isaiah 4:2; 11:1; 53:2; Jeremiah 23:5; 33:15; Zechariah 3:8; 6:12).

The Realization

In the book of Revelation, Jesus (who is a descendant of David) is described as "the Root of David" who reigns triumphantly as the eternal King (Revelation 5:5; 22:16).

16. SON OF MAN

"When the Son of Man comes in his glory, and all the angels with him, he will sit on his glorious throne." —Matthew 25:31

Prophecy

Prophecy can be defined simply at God speaking to and through a person. In this we see two types of prophecy: forthtelling and foretelling. Forthtelling is proclaiming a truth that God gives to the prophet—or to us. Foretelling is announcing a future event through the power of God.

The Reference

The prophet Daniel shares a vision about seeing "one like a son of man, coming with the clouds of heaven" and being "given authority, glory and sovereign power"; this ruler, whose kingdom is eternal, is worshiped by "all nations and peoples of every language" (Daniel 7:13–14).

The Realization

In the Gospels, Jesus often calls himself "the Son of Man" (Matthew 9:6; Mark 2:28; Luke 9:26; John 12:23). Before his crucifixion, he boldly proclaims to his accusers, "From now on you will see the Son of Man sitting at the right hand of the Mighty One and coming on the clouds of heaven" (Matthew 26:64).

Just before his return to heaven, Jesus tells his disciples, "All authority in heaven and on earth has been given to me" (Matthew 28:18). In the book of Revelation, people from every nation and language worship Jesus before his throne (Revelation 7:9–10).

17. THE BRIDEGROOM

"As a bridegroom rejoices over his bride, so will your God rejoice over you." —Isaiah 62:5

The Reference

The Old Testament uses a lot of marital imagery and symbolism to speak of God's relationship with his people—with God pictured as the groom and the people of God collectively as the bride (for example, Isaiah 54:5; Jeremiah 31:32; Hosea 1–3).

The Realization

Jesus also used this imagery and calls himself "the bridegroom" (Matthew 9:15). John says in the book of Revelation that "the wedding of the Lamb [Jesus] has come, and his bride [the church] has made herself ready" (Revelation 19:7).

Exhibit Hall 7

18. THE GREATER JONAH

"For as Jonah was three days and three nights in the belly of a huge fish, so the Son of Man will be three days and three nights in the heart of the earth." —Matthew 12:40

The Reference

In the Old Testament book of Jonah, we meet a harsh prophet who only reluctantly offers a message of judgment to those far from God—and this only after he spends three days and three nights praying inside the belly of a fish!

The Realization

In the New Testament, Jesus demonstrated compassion as he gladly and willingly offered a message of repentance and grace to those far from God (Mark 1:15; 6:34). Jesus, who spent three days and three nights in the grave, demonstrated he is the greater Jonah (Matthew 12:38–41).

19. THE PIERCED SAVIOR

"He was pierced for our rebellion, crushed for our sins. He was beaten so we could be whole. He was whipped so we could be healed." —Isaiah 53:5 NLT

The Reference

The Old Testament prophets Isaiah and Zechariah mention One who would be pierced—and *pierced for our benefit*, Isaiah adds (Isaiah 53:5; Zechariah 12:10).

The Realization

John records that this piercing took place at Jesus' crucifixion (John 19:33–34). When the disciple Thomas doubts Jesus' resurrection, he insists on seeing the nail holes in Jesus' hands, as well as his pierced side; when Thomas sees, he believes (John 20:25–29).

20. THE GOOD SHEPHERD

Jesus said, "I am the good shepherd. The good shepherd lays down his life for the sheep."
—John 10:11

The Reference

The Old Testament prophets often rebuke Israel's priests for being self-centered and evil shepherds of God's people (for example, Isaiah 56:11; Jeremiah 10:21; Ezekiel 34).

The Realization

In the New Testament, Jesus describes himself as the good shepherd of his followers (John 10:11–14). He is even called "the Chief Shepherd" (1 Peter 5:4) and the "great Shepherd of the sheep" (Hebrews 13:20).

THE GRAND FINALE AND BIG REVEAL

In Revelation, the Bible's last book, the apostle John is given a peek into the future and into eternity. God reveals to John—and to us—how Jesus is called by several descriptive titles and names that highlight Jesus' true nature.

- **The Alpha and the Omega** (Revelation 1:8; 21:6; 22:13)

  Alpha is the first letter of the Greek alphabet, *omega* the last—the equivalent of our A and Z. As Creator in the beginning and Judge at the end, Jesus forms the bookends of life.

- **The Lion of the tribe of Judah** (Revelation 5:5)

  While we sometimes think of Jesus as the Lamb of God, we don't often think of him as a lion. Yet he is both meek like a lamb and powerful like a lion.

- **The Word of God** (Revelation 19:13)

  Words explain, and Jesus explains God to a confused world (John 1:18).

- **King of Kings and Lord of Lords** (Revelation 19:16)

  Jesus is the ultimate ruler, leader, prophet, and Savior. Paul uses this same language in his first letter to Timothy (1 Timothy 6:15).

- **The bright Morning Star** (Revelation 22:16)

  Jesus pushes away the nighttime of darkness that envelops the world (John 8:12; 9:5; 2 Peter 1:19).

The Bible isn't just a story that *includes* Jesus. It's a story *about* Jesus. He does, in fact, show up throughout it, peeking out from the pages of Old Testament history, poetry, and prophecy.

If we read the Bible but somehow miss its emphasis on Jesus, we miss the point of the Bible.

PEEKING INTO THE FUTURE: HEAVEN, HELL, AND ETERNITY

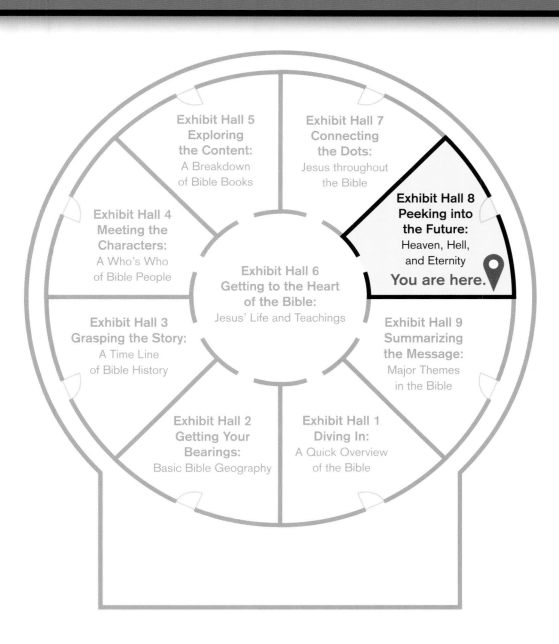

Exhibit Hall 5
Exploring
the Content:
A Breakdown
of Bible Books

Exhibit Hall 7
Connecting
the Dots:
Jesus throughout
the Bible

Exhibit Hall 8
Peeking into
the Future:
Heaven, Hell,
and Eternity
You are here.

Exhibit Hall 4
Meeting the
Characters:
A Who's Who
of Bible People

Exhibit Hall 6
Getting to the Heart
of the Bible:
Jesus' Life and Teachings

Exhibit Hall 3
Grasping the Story:
A Time Line
of Bible History

Exhibit Hall 9
Summarizing
the Message:
Major Themes
in the Bible

Exhibit Hall 2
Getting Your
Bearings:
Basic Bible Geography

Exhibit Hall 1
Diving In:
A Quick Overview
of the Bible

When a middle-class couple announces on their thirtieth anniversary that they are buying their dream cabin by a mountain stream in the Rockies, everyone is stunned. *No way!* people think. *They were both schoolteachers. They never earned great salaries, and they've always seemed to struggle financially. How is this possible?*

They tell their story. No, they didn't win the lottery; and no, they didn't receive a big inheritance. They acquired their nest egg the old-fashioned way. They worked hard, lived modestly, and squirreled away a chunk of every paycheck. With those savings they faithfully made wise investments—over a long, long time. This is how they're now paying cash for a quaint log home with a mountain view. Everyone who hears their story and sees pictures of their new future shakes his or her head—either in awe or in envy (or perhaps a little bit of both).

Instead of going through life living for the moment, this forward-thinking, extremely intentional couple ordered their lives around a future hope.

In a real sense, this is what the Bible wants us to do—take the long-term view. Beyond a focus on cabins and Colorado, real estate and retirement, we are to remember the link between the "now" and the "not yet." Why? Because what we do (or don't do) today—whether physically or spiritually—directly affects what our tomorrow will look like. It's only by facing our future that we are ever motivated to alter our present.

It's a constant tension, isn't it? Some people get so caught up in the moment, they become oblivious to future consequences (or opportunities). Others go to the opposite extreme. They get so obsessed with the future, they miss out on the wonder and beauty of life all around them. The Bible tells us to be wise and ever mindful of future realities without worrying or fretting over the future (Matthew 6:34; Luke 16:1–9).

We need to remember that the Bible is a story of life—the *true* story of life—that shows the world moving toward a certain conclusion. Because of that truth, this part of your *Self-Guided Tour of the Bible* will briefly describe four things that the Bible tells you about the future:

1. **The coming kingdom**
2. **The promise of resurrection**
3. **The certainty of judgment**
4. **The reality of heaven and hell**

1. The Coming Kingdom

Discussion of the kingdom of God starts in the Old Testament. Even though the Old Testament writers don't use the exact phrase "kingdom of God," they certainly grasp (and discuss) the concept.

- Isaiah speaks of one who will lead the people as their "Wonderful Counselor, Mighty God, Everlasting Father, Prince of Peace" (Isaiah 9:6).

- Ezekiel tells of a shepherd, like David, who will care for the people and will be their prince (Ezekiel 34:23–24).

- Jeremiah confirms that God will "raise up" one like King David who will be Israel's king (Jeremiah 30:9).

When Jesus was ministering on earth, he accepted and embraced his identity as Israel's king (Matthew 21:5; Mark 15:2; John 1:49). But he was not at all the kind of king the Jews of his time were expecting. They wanted an earthly ruler to deliver them once and for all from the tyrannical Roman Empire and to strengthen the nation of Israel. Jesus, however, came to deliver people—*all* people—from the oppression of sin and to reign eternally in their hearts. It's not surprising, then, that he talked often about "the kingdom of God" or "the kingdom of heaven."

Jesus declared, "The kingdom of God has come near" (Mark 1:15), even as he also urged his disciples to pray, "Your kingdom come" (Matthew 6:10). The fact that Christ said that the kingdom *has come* and then commanded his followers to pray for it *to come* shows the two aspects of the kingdom of God: now and not yet.

Now	Not Yet
Believers can surrender their lives to Jesus and allow him to rule over their lives *right now*, even as we live in a world that refuses to recognize or submit to Christ.	The Lord's rule on all the earth will be completely revealed in the future. We will experience the fullness of God's kingdom when Jesus Christ returns.

When Jesus first came to earth, only a few people were aware of his birth. His second coming will be a global phenomenon. Everyone will know when it happens. That's the day that Christ's kingdom will come in all its fullness. Every person will acknowledge Jesus as the eternal King. The whole world will know that Jesus "is Lord of lords and King of kings" (Revelation 17:14).

"At the name of Jesus every knee [will] bow, in heaven and on earth and under the earth." —Philippians 2:10

JESUS AND THE KINGDOM OF HEAVEN

The Gospel writer Matthew notes that when Jesus began his earthly ministry, he said much about "the kingdom of heaven"—the present and future rule of God.

Here's how Jesus described the kingdom of heaven in the Gospel of Matthew:

- It has come near (3:2; 4:17; 10:7).

- It belongs to "the poor in spirit" and to "those who are persecuted because of righteousness" (5:3, 10).

- It requires "righteousness [that] surpasses that of the Pharisees and the teachers of the law" (5:20).

- It has secrets and is misunderstood by many (13:11–23).

- It is like a field full of wheat and weeds (13:24–29).

- It is like a tiny mustard seed that grows to a great size (13:31–32).

- It is like yeast that permeates a whole batch of dough (13:33).

- It is like treasure hidden in a field or a pearl valuable beyond compare (13:44–46).

- It is like a net that catches good and bad fish (13:47–50).

- It is like a homeowner who brings new and old treasures out of a storage room (13:52).

- It is full of those who "become like little children" (18:3; 19:14).

- It is like a king who forgives servants who can't pay their debts (18:23–35).

- It is tough to enter for those who trust in their earthly riches (19:16–24).

- It is like a landowner who hires workers at different times and pays them the same wage (20:1–16).

- It is like a wedding reception that is opened up to the masses when the original invitees balk at attending (22:2–14).

- In the end days, it will be like ten maidens who are waiting for the bridegroom to show up, but half of them are ill-prepared and end up missing the wedding banquet (25:1–13).

Exhibit Hall 8

THE MEANING OF THE KINGDOM

Christians don't always agree when it comes to the meaning of the phrase the kingdom of God. Some people see the kingdom as a present spiritual rule in the hearts of the faithful because Jesus—through his death and resurrection—has already defeated sin and death. Others believe it refers to a future reign of Jesus on the earth—a literal, physical thousand-year reign, based on Revelation 20:1–7. Some think the kingdom of God has to do with the heavenly realm in which believers will spend eternity. Still other Bible readers understand it to mean some combination of these views. Regardless of the differing conclusions Christians may come to about the kingdom of God, it's important that we remember to honor Jesus as King of our lives and ruler of our hearts—both now and in the future.

Because of the reality of the kingdom of heaven (or the kingdom of God), the Bible urges followers of Jesus to live in this world without being of this world (1 John 2:15–16). We aren't to become enamored with worldly things that are passing away (1 John 2:17). Scripture reminds us that "our citizenship is in heaven" (Philippians 3:20), where Jesus himself is preparing our true home for us (John 14:1–4; Hebrews 11:8–10).

"All these people were still living by faith when they died. They did not receive the things promised; they only saw them and welcomed them from a distance, admitting that they were foreigners and strangers on earth. . . . They were longing for a better country—a heavenly one. Therefore God is not ashamed to be called their God, for he has prepared a city for them." —Hebrews 11:13–16

2. The Promise of Resurrection

The more you read the Bible, the more references you'll see to *resurrection*—that is, the dead coming back to life. This isn't merely a spiritual experience or a metaphorical expression; it's a physical reality. Resurrection in the Bible always involves the bringing back to life of real, flesh-and-blood bodies. As you read, you'll see three main ways the Bible speaks about resurrection:

1. **To speak of individuals who died and then miraculously received back their lives.** For example, God worked through the Old Testament prophets Elijah and Elisha to raise two boys from the dead (1 Kings 17:22; 2 Kings 4:32–37). Jesus went to a cemetery in Bethany and called Lazarus—buried for four days—out of the grave (John 11:1–44).

2. **To refer to Jesus coming out of the tomb**—literally and physically— on that first Easter morning (Matthew 28:1–10; Mark 16:1–8; Luke 24:1–49; John 20:1–23).

3. **To speak of the resurrection of all humanity at the end of time.** Jesus says in John 5:28–29 that there will be a resurrection of all the dead—the righteous to eternal life and the evil to eternal judgment. The apostle Paul repeats this idea: "There will be a resurrection of both the righteous and the wicked" (Acts 24:15).

Many assume that the life to come will be ethereal, that we'll be ghostly or angelic immaterial beings. The Bible, however, pictures a future that is gloriously solid and material.

"But in fact, Christ has been raised from the dead. He is the first of a great harvest of all who have died. So you see, just as death came into the world through a man, now the resurrection from the dead has begun through another man. Just as everyone dies because we all belong to Adam, everyone who belongs to Christ will be given new life. But there is an order to this resurrection: Christ was raised as the first of the harvest; then all who belong to Christ will be raised when he comes back."
—1 Corinthians 15:20–23 NLT

As the prototype of resurrected humans, Jesus is proof positive that our resurrection bodies will be physical yet fit for eternity. Like Jesus' body after his resurrection, our resurrected bodies will be seeable and touchable (John 20:20–27), yet "they will be raised as spiritual bodies" (1 Corinthians 15:44 NLT).

3. The Certainty of Judgment

Throughout the Bible, God is addressed and described by his many roles.

- Creator (Isaiah 40:28)
- Maker (Psalm 95:6)
- Lord (Psalm 39:7)
- King (Psalm 47:6–7)
- Helper (Hebrews 13:6)
- Savior (Isaiah 43:3)
- Father (Romans 1:7)
- Judge (Genesis 18:25; Psalms 94:2; 96:13; 98:9; Romans 2:16)

God as Judge is not a thought many people like to entertain. But it's a fact that the Bible repeats again and again. Ultimately, when the Bible speaks of judgment, it refers to a future day when the Creator will convene a kind of heavenly court. All the resurrected ones (every person who has ever lived) will be summoned to appear.

The Bible says that every human being will come face-to-face with the Lord at the end of time. Whether we call this judgment day, the day of reckoning, a time of accounting, a review of our lives, or something else, the fact remains that we will each have an appointment with God.

Scripture provides ample warning of this day:

- "We will all stand before God's judgment seat" (Romans 14:10).
- "We must all appear before the judgment seat of Christ, so that each of us may receive what is due us for the things done while in the body, whether good or bad" (2 Corinthians 5:10).
- "Then I saw a great white throne and him who was seated on it. The earth and the heavens fled from his presence, and there was no place for them. And I saw the dead, great and small, standing before the throne, and books were opened. Another book was opened, which is the book of life. The dead were judged according to what they had done as recorded in the books. The sea gave up the dead that were in it, and death and Hades gave up the dead that were in them, and each person was judged according to what they had done. Then death and Hades were thrown into the lake of fire. The lake of fire is the second death. Anyone whose name was

not found written in the book of life was thrown into the lake of fire" (Revelation 20:11–15).

No one knows exactly what this time of judgment will look like. But one thing we know for sure is that judgment for unbelievers and believers will be vastly different.

How will unbelievers experience judgment? Those who dismiss Jesus (and reject his sacrifice on their behalf) will consequently be judged by how well they have lived up to God's holy standards. Anyone falling short of God's glorious standard of perfection will experience the terrible sentence of eternal separation from God (Romans 3:23; Revelation 20:11–15).

What does judgment look like for believers? Because Jesus has already experienced divine judgment for the sins of his followers, those who've trusted Christ to be their Savior (and substitute) have already had their sin judged—as well as paid for and removed—by Jesus' death on the cross (1 John 2:2). He took our sins upon himself and then absorbed the punishment that we deserved (1 Peter 2:24). In exchange, Christ gave believers his righteousness (2 Corinthians 5:21). Fully pardoned and possessing eternal life, Christians are now children of God who don't have to worry about punishment and don't have to wonder about their ultimate destiny (John 1:12; 5:24). Christians can joyfully say:

> **"We will not be afraid on the day of judgment, but we can face [God] with confidence because we live like Jesus here in this world." —1 John 4:17 NLT**

This means judgment for believers will not be about where we will spend eternity. It will be an evaluation of how faithfully we have served Christ on the earth (2 Corinthians 5:10). Several New Testament passages speak of eternal rewards, which suggests that obedience in this life will somehow affect our "service opportunities" in the life to come (Matthew 5:12; Mark 9:41; 2 Timothy 4:8; Revelation 22:12).

4. The Reality of Heaven and Hell

Heaven is described in the Old Testament as a place where God dwells and where his throne is located (Deuteronomy 26:15; 1 Kings 8:39; Psalm 11:4; Isaiah 66:1).

In the New Testament, it's pictured as a place where:

- Christians receive rewards (Matthew 5:12).
- Christians find everlasting security (Matthew 6:20).
- There is great "rejoicing" (Luke 15:7).
- There are "many rooms" (John 14:2).
- All of God's creatures worship him with abandon before his throne (Revelation 5:13).
- God dwells with his people in the Holy City—the beautiful New Jerusalem that comes "down out of heaven" (Revelation 21:2–3).

Perhaps the most telling descriptive phrase of eternity is found in Revelation 21:1, where the apostle John writes of seeing "a new heaven and a new earth." The Greek word John uses for *new* is a word that means "superior" or "of a better quality." It's not as if we'll exist in a wholly different realm or a quasi-nether world. Heaven will be God's original creation, *this* world, only restored and made better than it was to begin with. From reading John's words, you get the sense that heaven will be earth, and earth will be heaven.

THINGS THE BIBLE *NEVER* SAYS ABOUT HEAVEN

- ❖ Heaven is located in the sky or in the clouds.
- ❖ Everyone goes to heaven when they die.
- ❖ People, if they're good on earth, become angels in heaven.
- ❖ We will sit around and sing or play musical instruments for all eternity in heaven.
- ❖ The residents of heaven are disembodied, ghostly spirits.

The apostle John says it will be a place free from death, sorrow, crying, and pain:

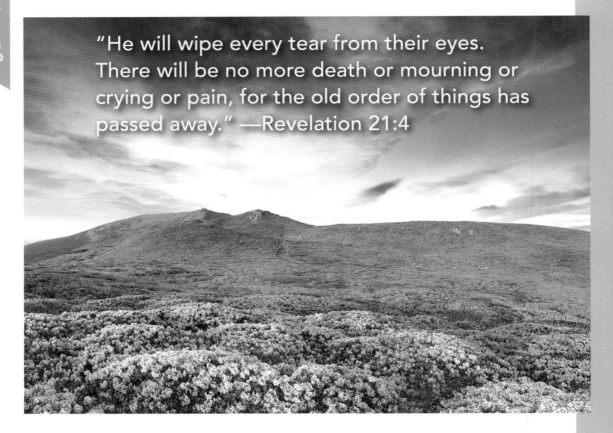

"He will wipe every tear from their eyes. There will be no more death or mourning or crying or pain, for the old order of things has passed away." —Revelation 21:4

We will have glorified physical bodies, and we will inhabit a new earth. We won't be transparent, ghostlike beings. A mysterious but *real* future awaits us.

The alternative to heaven, according to the Bible, is a place called *hell*. Not a lot of people want to think or talk about it, but it's a frequent subject in Scripture. What's more, Jesus talked extensively about hell. The Bible speaks of hell as a literal place of separation from God (2 Thessalonians 1:9). Jesus described it as a place of intolerable suffering (Matthew 13:42, 49–50; 24:51; 25:30). There is no hope in hell (Luke 16:19–31). There is no light there (Matthew 22:13). There is no rest there (Revelation 14:11). Though cartoons often depict hell as a big party, the Bible suggests it is a place of abject loneliness, free from camaraderie (Luke 16:22–23). Jesus used the adjective "eternal" to describe hell (Matthew 18:8; 25:41, 46).

Here are two things every Bible reader (experienced or rookie) needs to remember about hell:

1. God doesn't want anyone to end up there.

In the Old Testament we read, "As surely as I live, declares the Sovereign LORD, I take no pleasure in the death of the wicked, but rather that they turn from their ways and live. Turn! Turn from your evil ways!" (Ezekiel 33:11). The New Testament repeats this idea. We read there that God "wants all people to be saved and to come to a knowledge of the truth" (1 Timothy 2:4). We see that God "does not want anyone to be destroyed, but wants everyone to repent" (2 Peter 3:9 NLT).

THE FLAMES OF HELL?

In talking about the future punishment of the wicked, Jesus often used the Greek word *Gehenna* (translated as "hell"; Matthew 5:22, 29–30; 10:28; 18:8–9; Mark 9:43–47; Luke 12:5). This was a reference to the Valley of Ben Hinnom, a ravine adjacent to Jerusalem that was the site of ancient pagan practices, including child sacrifice, where people would "burn their sons and daughters in the fire" (Jeremiah 7:31; 2 Kings 23:10; 2 Chronicles 28:3).

Will hell be a place of literal fire? Christians disagree over whether Bible verses describing hell as a place of fire are meant to be interpreted literally. Yet the imagery of fire gives us a graphic picture of what eternity will be like for those who reject the grace of God.

2. God has made provision for everyone to avoid hell.

In sending his Son, Jesus, to die for our sins and to be judged in our place, God showed his great love for us (John 3:16; 1 John 4:10). Our debt has been paid. Our pardon has been purchased. But a pardon that's not accepted is of no value whatsoever.

The Curious Story of George Wilson

In December of 1829, George Wilson and James Porter robbed a United States mail carrier in Pennsylvania. Both men were caught, tried, and found guilty of six charges that included robbery of the mail "and putting the life of the driver in jeopardy." The following May both men were sentenced to death by hanging.

By today's standards, such justice seems unusually harsh, since no one was killed during the robbery. Nevertheless, this death sentence was the ruling of the court.

Porter was put to death on schedule. Wilson, however, was not. Just before his execution date, a number of Wilson's influential friends pleaded on his behalf for mercy from President Andrew Jackson. Sure enough, President Jackson issued a presidential pardon for the charges that had resulted in the death sentence. This meant Wilson would have to serve only a twenty-year prison term for his other crimes.

Incredibly, Wilson refused the pardon!

According to the official report, Wilson was returned to court as prosecutors attempted to "force" the pardon on him. He instead rejected the pardon and refused to speak.

Wilson's case went all the way to the Supreme Court. The attorney general made the following comments: "The court cannot give the prisoner the benefit of the pardon, unless he claims the benefit of it... It is his property; and he may accept it or not, as he pleases" (United States v. George Wilson. 32 U.S. 150).

Inexplicably, despite having access to a pardon, Wilson chose execution instead.

In Christ, God offers a pardon to sinful people. If you have never put your faith in Christ, why not do so right now? How do you do that? There's no formula, no magical prayer. Simply thank God for sending Christ. Admit that you have sinned—confess to God all the ways you have rebelled against him. Acknowledge your need for forgiveness and your desire to have new life—real, eternal life. Tell God that you believe that Christ's death was for you and that you trust his sacrifice to count for you. Tell him you want the pardon he's provided and his free gift of salvation (Ephesians 2:8–9).

"For God so loved the world that he gave his one and only Son, that whoever believes in him shall not perish but have eternal life." —John 3:16

One of the marks of a wise person is the ability to look ahead, see danger or opportunity, and adjust accordingly. People who do this with their finances might one day get to enjoy a mountain home for a few fleeting years. But those who do this in the spiritual realm—listening carefully to what the Bible says about things to come and responding with humility and faith—will have joy unending.

"And now, dear children, continue in [Christ], so that when he appears we may be confident and unashamed before him at his coming." —1 John 2:28

The Bible is crystal clear: The day of Christ's appearing is just ahead. In light of that future certainty, let's live *this* day with *that* day in view.

SUMMARIZING THE MESSAGE: MAJOR THEMES IN THE BIBLE

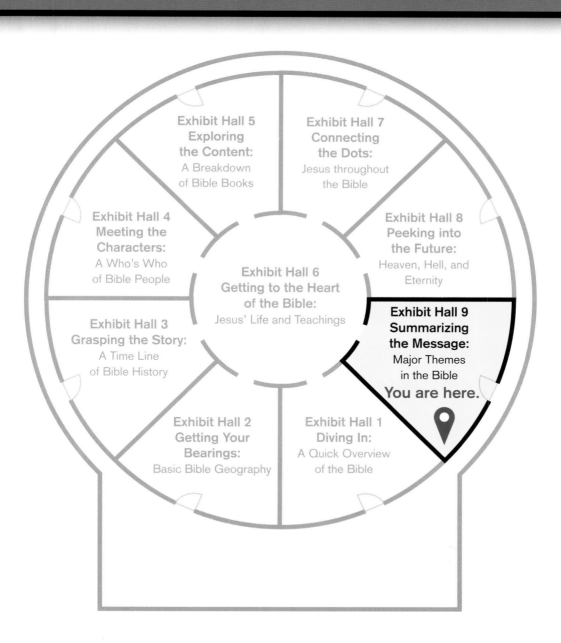

Exhibit Hall 5
Exploring
the Content:
A Breakdown
of Bible Books

Exhibit Hall 7
Connecting
the Dots:
Jesus throughout
the Bible

Exhibit Hall 4
Meeting the
Characters:
A Who's Who
of Bible People

Exhibit Hall 6
Getting to the Heart
of the Bible:
Jesus' Life and Teachings

Exhibit Hall 8
Peeking into
the Future:
Heaven, Hell, and
Eternity

Exhibit Hall 3
Grasping the Story:
A Time Line
of Bible History

Exhibit Hall 9
Summarizing
the Message:
Major Themes
in the Bible
You are here.

Exhibit Hall 2
Getting Your
Bearings:
Basic Bible Geography

Exhibit Hall 1
Diving In:
A Quick Overview
of the Bible

Bible scholars have suggested that when you boil it down, the Bible *really* only contains a handful of big ideas, which begs the question: Do we really need sixty-six books that fill over one thousand pages?

The short answer is *yes!* Through all those great Bible stories and characters, God keeps repeating a handful of themes. There are a couple of good reasons for all this repetition. First, humans are hard of hearing. Second, we are prone to forget.

Here in this part of your *Self-Guided Tour of the Bible*, we want to point out eight central ideas that permeate the Bible. We'll introduce them (not exhaust them). We'll quickly show why each theme is significant. We'll give a few examples from God's Word. And we'll show how Jesus is connected to each of these themes. Remember: Since Christ is the centerpiece of Scripture, every one of these big, sweeping ideas finds its source and meaning in him.

Here are the eight themes we'll briefly explore:

1. **God *is*.** (The reality of God)

2. **God is awesome!** (The glory of God)

3. **People are broken.** (The sinfulness of humanity)

4. **God rescues us in Christ.** (The wonder of salvation)

5. **We live by faith.** (The call to believe)

6. **This world is not all there is.** (The reality of the kingdom of heaven)

7. **Life is a team sport.** (The necessity of community)

8. **All will be well.** (The promise of restoration)

1. God *is.*

One major idea that permeates the Bible is *the reality of God*. The Bible begins with God. When nothing else is, God is: "In the beginning God . . ." (Genesis 1:1). In the first verse of the Bible, God is revealed as Creator. If you flip to the very end of the Bible—the book of Revelation, the apostle John's vision of heaven and eternity—God is revealed as King, Lord, and Judge of all the earth (Revelation 15:3; 20:12–13).

In between Genesis and Revelation, the words *God* and *Lord* are mentioned thousands of times. Clearly, from beginning to end, the reality of God is a dominating idea in the Bible.

In the Old Testament, God is often perceived as invisible or hidden in dramatic displays of fire and smoke (Exodus 19:18). His power, wisdom, and holiness caused people to tremble with fear and awe at his presence (Exodus 20:18; Psalms 96:9; 119:120; Proverbs 28:14). But people who enjoyed a close relationship with God also experienced him and his love in extremely personal ways. Adam and Eve, for example, spent time *with* God in the garden; after their fateful choice to disobey him, they tried to physically hide from God's presence (Genesis 3:8). The Bible describes Abraham as God's "friend" (2 Chronicles 20:7; Isaiah 41:8; James 2:23). Moses is a great example of someone who experienced God's presence, love, and friendship firsthand (Exodus 34:5–6). God himself "would speak to Moses face to face, as one speaks to a friend" (Exodus 33:11).

In the New Testament, we are introduced to Jesus, the Son of God. Though this carpenter-turned-teacher from Nazareth claimed repeatedly to *be* God, he was visible and approachable (John 8:56–59; 10:30–33)! He came close enough to be seen, heard, and touched (1 John 1:1–3).

After his death, burial, resurrection, and return to heaven, Jesus sent the very Spirit of God to live in the hearts and souls of his followers (Acts 2). What a jaw-dropping reality! Think about it: The Gospels in the New Testament show God *among* us (John 1:14). Jesus was "God *with* us" (Matthew 1:23, emphasis added). The book of Acts in the New Testament shows that the Spirit is God *in* us.

WHY IS THIS BIBLICAL THEME SO IMPORTANT?

If the Bible is true (and, of course, we believe it is), then God *is*. God exists. We're not alone in the universe. The world and the human race are not cosmic accidents, the result of eons of time + chance + nothing. We were designed. We were made for a purpose. The world is not random; it is going somewhere. We have meaning and significance.

TRINITY

The Bible reveals God as existing eternally as three distinct persons: Father, Son, and Holy Spirit. The mystery is that we worship one God (not multiple gods), yet each of the three divine Persons is fully God (not a piece or part or form of God). The oneness of God is stated in Deuteronomy 6:4: "The LORD, our God, the LORD is one." The "threeness" of God is seen in passages like:

- Matthew 3:16–17 where the Father speaks and the Spirit descends as Jesus is baptized;

- John 14:16 where Jesus speaks of asking the Father to send the Spirit;

- Matthew 28:18–20 where Jesus speaks of baptizing new believers "in the name of the Father and of the Son and of the Holy Spirit";

- 2 Corinthians 13:14 which is a prayer/benediction that mentions the grace of Jesus, the love of God, and the fellowship of the Holy Spirit.

Though Scripture never uses the word *Trinity*, it's a helpful term for explaining the three-in-one God we meet in the Bible.

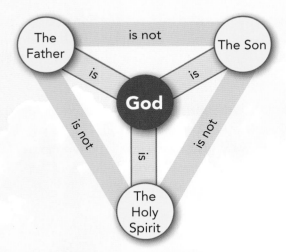

This helpful diagram illustrates what Scripture reveals about how there is one God, yet the three Persons of God are distinct. For example, the Son *is* God, but the Son *is not* the Holy Spirit and the Son *is not* the Father.

2. God is awesome!

A second big idea that observant Bible readers will notice as they read through the Bible is *the glory of God;* in other words, God's awesomeness.

People toss around the word *awesome* a lot: "That game-winning play was awesome!" "That sandwich was awesome!" But in the strictest sense, the word *awesome* means far more than having your taste buds tantalized. Being *awed* means to be filled with speechless wonder. It means to be breathless with holy fear. When we are in the presence of true awesomeness, we hug the ground, tremble, freeze, even lose the power of speech.

HOLINESS

Exiled on the island of Patmos, the apostle John had a strange vision of four creatures surrounding the throne of God in heaven, chanting: "Holy, holy, holy is the Lord God Almighty" (Revelation 4:1–8). In the Old Testament, the prophet Isaiah saw a similar vision (Isaiah 6:1–7). Holiness is another awesome characteristic of God. Holy means "perfect, without defect." It means that God is completely set apart from all sin or evil. As the Holy One, God stands unique. No one else is like him.

Hundreds of Bible verses describe God's awesomeness as his *glory*. In Hebrew (the language used to write most of the Old Testament), the word *glory* means "weighty" or "heavy." God isn't an insignificant character. He's not hiding off in the margins of life, resting lightly on people and events. His majesty is central to everything; his splendor fills the universe. There's a divine beauty that covers the world like a heavy blanket. It's there, even when we don't feel it, even if we never acknowledge it.

Question: In what specific ways is God awesome? Answer: In more ways than we can mention. But let's take a minute and list seven "heavy," breathtaking truths the Bible reveals about our awesome God:

1. **God is infinite**. He is without end or limits (1 Kings 8:27; Psalm 145:3).

2. **God is eternal**. He is outside of and unbounded by time (Genesis 21:33; Psalm 90:2).

3. **God is all-knowing**. He sees and comprehends all things—both actual and possible (Psalms 139:1–4; 147:4–5; Hebrews 4:13; 1 John 3:20).

4. **God is all-powerful**. Nothing is too hard for the Almighty (Job 42:2; Jeremiah 32:17; Matthew 19:26).

5. **God is present everywhere**. There is no place where he is not (Psalm 139:7–12; Jeremiah 23:23–24).

6. **God is sovereign**. He authoritatively rules and orchestrates all things for his glory and the good of the creatures he loves (Ephesians 1:4–14, 21).

7. **God is unchanging**. He doesn't morph or evolve; he is reliable and consistent (Psalm 102:27; Malachi 3:6; James 1:17).

WHY IS THIS BIBLICAL THEME SO IMPORTANT?

By constantly showing God as glorious, the Bible makes it clear that he is worth not only our attention but also our devotion. Because God is awesome, he deserves all the honor we can give him. We should spend our lives making much of God. We should order our lives around him.

In truth *this* is what worship is. Our English word *worship* means the state of having worth. Worship isn't merely a church service or singing religious songs. It can be that, but it is *so* much more. Worship is about what we treat as worthy or valuable 24/7. People worship money, fame, power, beauty—all kinds of things. But because God alone is truly awesome, we should worship him and not lesser things.

3. People are broken.

A third big idea that's impossible to miss as you examine the Bible is *the sinfulness of humanity*. Scripture begins in Genesis with a description of creation and then briefly shows the first man and woman enjoying an idyllic life in Eden. They have complete access to God (who, as we've just seen, is the embodiment of awesome). They have unimaginable freedom. Life, as the saying goes, is good!

But even with all this blessing, the first couple inexplicably listens to the tempter and violates the one restriction God has placed on them. Their eating of forbidden fruit isn't a mistake, a slipup, or an accident. It is a flagrant act of rebellion.

Adam and Eve's sin results in catastrophic consequences: Guilt. Fear. Shame. Separation from God. Death. Forced to leave Eden, they live with the daily reminders of their rebellion against their Maker. And because of their sin, their children—and their children's children, and every human that has been born ever since (other than Jesus Christ)—also face the consequences for their own rebellion against God. This inherited rebelliousness is called our *sinful nature*.

The rest of the Bible vividly demonstrates how, as sons and daughters of Adam and Eve, we are "chips off the old block."

- The first child born into the world, Cain, ends up murdering the second, Abel (Genesis 4:8).

- Soon after that, the Bible declares that "every inclination of the thoughts of the human heart was only evil all the time" (Genesis 6:5). God sends a flood to judge such evil. Only one family (Noah's family) survives. Guess what? They bring sin with them into the post-flood world!

- After being delivered by God from Egypt via dramatic miracles, it's only a matter of weeks before the tribes of Israel are bowing down to a golden idol shaped like a calf (Exodus 32)!

- What about the spiritual climate during the time of the Judges? Wide-scale love for God? A desire to do his will? No. National lawlessness—"everyone did as they saw fit" (Judges 17:6).

- The Bible makes it clear that no one is exempt. *All people* are sinful and broken. Even the great King David, the one described as "a man after [God's] own heart" (1 Samuel 13:14), becomes guilty of adultery and murder (2 Samuel 11).

■ In the New Testament it's more of the same. Religious leaders plot to kill Jesus after he defies Jewish tradition by performing undeniable miracles of great compassion on the Sabbath (Mark 3:1–6). Roman soldiers take delight in beating, mocking, and spitting on Jesus (Mark 15:19). People are "lovers of themselves" (2 Timothy 3:2). No wonder the apostle Paul writes, "All have sinned and fall short of the glory of God" (Romans 3:23).

SIN To sin means to disobey God, to do wrong, or to fall short of God's expectations for us. We sin when we choose something else over God. And that disobedience separates us from him. Despite how hard we try or how badly we want to not sin, we still do. We can't help it. Every human inherits a sinful nature from Adam and Eve. The Bible says that if we claim we don't sin, we're lying (1 John 1:8).

WHY IS THIS BIBLICAL THEME SO IMPORTANT?

We are made in the glorious image of God, but we are fallen. We were created to reflect God's nature and relate to him. Instead, we resent and resist his rule over our lives. In short then, we are messy masterpieces, glorious ruins. As creatures bearing the image of God, we possess great dignity. But sin has brought degradation. When the first humans walked away from the One who is life, human nature experienced death. When Adam and Eve first severed their ties with the One who gives meaning to the universe, all humanity lost their sense of meaning. All this to say, we are *not* okay. We are badly broken. We are in trouble. We can't save ourselves. But, thankfully, there's another huge theme to counteract this bad news.

4. God rescues us in Christ.

Another towering idea that looms over the pages of the story of the Bible is *the wonder of salvation*. God relentlessly seeks to find us when we are lost, forgive us when we sin, and fix us when we are broken. This is seen in the Bible from the first page to the last.

- Almost before Adam and Eve have swallowed the forbidden fruit, we see God coming into the Garden of Eden, calling out to his cowering creatures, "Where are you?" (Genesis 3:9). Then, even as God confronts Adam and Eve with their sin, he mentions that one of Eve's descendants will crush the head of the serpent, the one who has deceptively introduced such evil and suffering into the world (Genesis 3:15).

- Soon after, Noah is a recipient of God's favor (i.e., his grace, Genesis 6:8). As a result, he and his family are brought safely through the great flood.

- In Exodus, God delivers his people from Egyptian bondage.

- In Judges, God repeatedly rescues the Israelites from oppression at the hands of neighboring nations.

- In the psalms, David makes a frequent point of mentioning all the ways and times God has come to his aid.

- In the book of Jonah, we see God command one of his prophets to travel to Nineveh (the capital city of ancient Assyria) and urge the people there to turn from their sin or face judgment. It's not as though the Assyrians are seeking God. They're not. They worship other gods and are bent on destroying the Israelites. Even so, God proactively sends a messenger to warn them. When they repent, they are spared.

In each of these instances, short-term physical deliverance is a picture of the eternal and spiritual salvation God wants to bring to his people. In his compassion and love, God pursues people and desires to save them from the consequences of their own rebellion (Psalm 103:8–18; Jonah 4:2).

And this pursuit continues in the New Testament.

- The New Testament Gospels depict Jesus Christ as the "sent" one of God (John 5:24). In Jesus' own words, "The Son of Man came to seek and save the lost" (Luke 19:10). His invitation? "Come to me" (Matthew 11:28). His legacy? "God demonstrates his own love for us in this: While we were still sinners, Christ died for us" (Romans 5:8).

- In Acts 9, we read the astounding story of Saul (a.k.a. the apostle Paul). He is dead set on wiping off the map the new Jesus movement. He is hell-bent on rounding up Christians, and he is violently opposed to this new entity called the church—until the day Jesus essentially *hunts* him down (and *knocks* him down, literally!) on the Damascus Road. From that day forward, Paul becomes a partner with Christ in the mission of going to the ends of the earth to bring people to God.

Throughout its pages, the Bible shows God as pursuing and wooing his wayward creatures. In the Gospels, we see Jesus going, preaching, warning, inviting, calling, and training a group to take his message to the world. We see him compassionately serving, healing, and accepting people—including people on the fringes of society who are ignored or disdained by others. In the end we see him suffering, dying, rising, and calling his followers to "Go!"—go and tell others about Jesus. Why this theme of rescue? Why such divine passion for a relationship with indifferent people? Because of who God is.

- **God is loving**. This means he always seeks the best for his creatures (John 3:16; 1 John 4:7–21).

- **God is compassionate**. This means his heart is moved when he sees the ones he loves in trouble (Psalm 103:2–4; 145:8; Matthew 9:36).

- **God is merciful**. This means God spares us from the punishment we deserve (Nehemiah 9:31; Luke 6:36).

- **God is gracious**. This means God gives us amazingly good things we don't deserve (Psalm 116:5). Grace is undeserved favor (Ephesians 2:8–9). Perhaps the best New Testament picture of grace is the story of the Prodigal Son (Luke 15:11–32). It's hard to read this story and not be blown away by God's heart.

- **God is forgiving**. This means God blots out our sins (Psalm 86:5; Ephesians 1:7). In Christ, our offenses against God are paid for and wiped away. When we trust in Christ and what he did for us at the cross, we are made right with God. Jesus takes upon himself the sin of all who believe. In exchange he gives his perfect righteousness to all who humbly trust in him.

SALVATION

Salvation literally means "deliverance from destruction, difficulty, or evil." In the most basic sense, salvation is rescue from something bad, such as vicious enemies (Psalm 7:1) or a violent storm (Matthew 8:25). Spiritually speaking, salvation occurs when God saves us from a life without him. Salvation is being spared the eternal punishment we actually deserve because of our disobedience. Instead of punishment, salvation means we receive blessing. As you read the Bible, observe the repeated idea that salvation is a gift of God (John 4:10; Romans 6:23). We don't deserve it, and we could never earn it. It's offered in grace. We receive salvation by faith (Ephesians 2:8–9)—faith in Jesus Christ (John 3:16; Romans 10:13). What's more, the Bible declares that spiritual salvation is found only in Jesus (John 14:6; Acts 4:12).

WHY IS THIS BIBLICAL THEME SO IMPORTANT?

The consistent message of the Bible is that God's heart is for sinners—which is every one of us! God hates sin because he is holy and because sin kills the ones he loves. The coming of Jesus into the world is the clearest proof of God's love. The death of Christ shows the lengths God will go to in order to solve our problem of sin and bring us back to himself. God is not only *eager* to save; he is *able* to save!

5. We live by faith.

A fifth major theme of the Bible—we see it from start to finish—is *the call to believe*. Having faith in God means trusting him completely and obediently doing what he asks us to do—even when we don't understand his reasons. In the Bible, there are many examples of God calling people to do some rather unusual things. Yet they trust what God says, obey his call to believe, and are rewarded for it.

- At God's "strange" command, Noah builds a massive boat for a massive flood that God says is coming. Noah and his family are the only people saved from a great flood (Genesis 6–9).

- At God's "odd" command, Abraham packs his bags and heads west and then south (Genesis 12). No doubt, lots of people think the old man is nuts. God, however, praises his great faith and lavishes world-changing blessings on him (Galatians 3:6).

- At God's "bizarre" command, Moses and the Israelites—being chased by the Egyptian army—walk straight toward the Red Sea. As they reach the shoreline, God opens a passageway right through the water (Exodus 14).

- At God's "crazy" command, Joshua and the Israelite army march around the walled city of Jericho and then shout—and the walls topple (Joshua 6).

The importance of faith continues throughout the Old Testament—in story after story and book after book.

- David (the king-in-waiting and target of King Saul's vicious envy) continually places his trust in God and is delivered. Psalms 27, 56, and 62 are just three examples of David expressing his faith.

- When David's son Solomon decides to compile all his best wisdom in a book, he writes, "Trust in the LORD with all your heart and lean not on your own understanding; in all your

FAITH

Many people view *faith* as an abstract collection of spiritual ideas. The problem with this idea is that in the Bible, faith isn't portrayed as merely a collection of thoughts about God. On the contrary, it's pictured as an active trust *in* God. In the Bible, faith is walking *with* God into and through the unknown and uneasy stretches of life. Faith isn't a noun; it's a verb. It's boldly believing and doing whatever God says.

ways submit to him, and he will make your paths straight" (Proverbs 3:5–6). Later he warns, "Those who trust in themselves are fools" (Proverbs 28:26).

- The prophet Daniel—rather than comply with the evil commands of the Medo-Persian king—trusts God to protect him when the king has him thrown into a den of hungry lions (Daniel 6).

And this relentless stress on faith fills the New Testament as well.

- In the Gospels, Jesus hammers away at our need to believe (John 6:35). He *rebukes* his followers when they fail to trust (Matthew 14:31). He *marvels* at outsiders who exercise great faith (Luke 7:9).

- The writer of Hebrews devotes a whole chapter to people who trusted God in courageous ways (Hebrews 11).

- James goes so far as to say a so-called faith that is all talk and no action isn't really faith at all (James 2:14–26).

WHY IS THIS BIBLICAL THEME SO IMPORTANT?

Faith is important, because faith is how God saves us (Ephesians 2:8–9; also see theme #4). Being right with God is not about *trying* to please God; it's about *trusting* in Jesus, who perfectly pleased God always. According to the Bible, we don't need enormous faith (Luke 17:6). All that is required is a tiny bit of faith—in the right person. And if our faith is small, the Lord can make it grow (Matthew 17:17–20; Luke 17:5). It's when we live by faith that we please God (Hebrews 11:6).

6. This world is not all there is.

A sixth theme that's prominent in God's Word is *the reality of the kingdom of heaven* (the kingdom of God).

This physical world in which we find ourselves is not all there is to reality. There is more to this life than just this life. We now live a material existence, but there is also an invisible but entirely real spiritual dimension to life.

All through the Bible we read about moments when God "pulls back the curtains," as it were, to reveal a realm that transcends human comprehension and experience. Consider, for example, the following events described in the Bible.

- In Genesis 28, Jacob dreams at Bethel and sees angels ascending and descending a stairway to heaven. We know this isn't just a case of having eaten too much spicy food at bedtime because Jacob wakes up and makes this classic statement: "Surely the LORD is in this place, and I was not aware of it" (verse 16).

- In Exodus 24, Moses, Aaron, the elders of Israel, and Aaron's two sons go up to a mountain to feast in the majestic presence of God.

- In 2 Kings 6, the prophet Elisha prays that his alarmed servant's eyes will be opened to spiritual realities. Suddenly the young man is able to see heavenly chariots of fire and horses surrounding them (verse 17).

- In his book, the prophet Ezekiel records vision after vision of eternal realities that defy description. He describes four unusual living creatures—each with four faces and four wings and each having a human form—that were accompanied by wheels (Ezekiel 1:4–24). Later Ezekiel sees bones that join together, become covered in flesh, and come to life when he speaks to them (Ezekiel 37:1–14).

- In Luke 2, in the New Testament, a few shepherds are minding their own business when the nighttime skies above them suddenly blaze with the light of an angelic army. With excitement, these heavenly messengers announce the birth of "a Savior . . . the Messiah, the Lord" (verse 11). After praising God, the angels disappear and the skies darken again.

- Beginning his ministry, Jesus announces the arrival of "the kingdom of God" (Mark 1:15). Later, he clarifies that his kingdom is not necessarily visible or earthly (Luke 17:20–21; John 18:36).

- In 2 Corinthians 12, the apostle Paul speaks of a man (likely himself) who was caught up into heaven ("paradise," verse 4).

- In the book of Revelation, the apostle John is given a front-row seat and a preview of the future hope Christians have. John sees into the last days of the world and into heaven itself. You get the sense he keeps rubbing his eyes as he struggles to find words to express all that he sees.

WHY IS THIS BIBLICAL THEME SO IMPORTANT?

We all have deep, inexpressible longings in our souls, a sense that there is more to life than meets the eye. Some have called this an ache for transcendence, even an eternal homesickness. In his book *Mere Christianity*, C. S. Lewis put it this way: "If I find in myself desires which nothing in this world can satisfy, the only logical explanation is that I was made for another world."

The spiritual life is about developing "the eyes of [our] heart" (Ephesians 1:18). As we do that, we are able to remember that this world is passing away and that our true home is in heaven. This helps us avoid the great trap of becoming overly attached to stuff that cannot last.

7. Life is a team sport.

A seventh key theme that's front and center all the way through the Bible is *the necessity of community*. It almost doesn't matter where you turn in the Bible: God's Word makes it clear that we humans were made for relationships. We need one another. We were never meant to "do life" all by ourselves. Here are just a few examples from the Bible about our need for a team.

- Before the creation of Eve, we hear God say about the solitary Adam, "It is not good for the man to be alone" (Genesis 2:18).

- In Exodus 3–4, when God calls Moses to go and lead the Hebrew people out of Egypt, Moses confesses his insecurity and uncertainty. God responds by giving him an assistant—Moses' brother, Aaron.

- Later in Exodus 18, when Moses is trying to be the one-man judicial system for between two and three million people, his father-in-law, Jethro, urges him to put together a team of judges—or risk burning out.

- When King David rises to power, he surrounds himself with a team comprised of the prophet Nathan, assorted military experts, secretaries, priests, and advisors (2 Samuel 7:1–3; 8:15–18).

- In Ecclesiastes 4:9–12, we read: "Two are better than one, because they have a good return for their labor: if either of them falls down, one can help the other up. But pity anyone who falls and has no one to help them up. Also, if two lie down together, they will keep warm. But how can one keep warm alone? Though one may be overpowered, two can defend themselves. A cord of three strands is not quickly broken."

- In the New Testament Gospels, we see that even Jesus doesn't try to "go it alone." He immediately gathers a small group of followers, and they go everywhere together (Mark 3:13–18).

- In Mark 2:1–12, we read the great story of a group of devoted friends who bring their paralyzed buddy to Jesus so that he might experience healing.

- In Matthew 26:36–46, on the darkest night of his life, Jesus asks Peter, James, and John, his three closest friends, to pray with him. Even though his friends aren't exceptionally helpful, the Son of God's example illustrates the importance of "doing life together" with other people.

- In the book of Acts, we see believers in the early church living in community. They spend time together eating, sharing, learning, and praising God (Acts 2:42–47). They do this daily—not just once a week on Sunday morning.

- In Romans 12:3–8 and 1 Corinthians 12:12–31, the apostle Paul uses the metaphor of a human body with all its individual parts to picture the way in which Jesus wants his church to function. We aren't to go through life with an independent mind-set but an interdependent one.

Even though the word *community* doesn't appear much in the New Testament, the concept permeates the Gospels and epistles. The New Testament writers often teach the importance of community by using words such as "unity" and "same mind" (Ephesians 1:10; 4:3, 13; Philippians 4:2; Colossians 3:14) and giving a host of commands about how followers of Jesus are to treat one another (Romans 12:10; 1 Corinthians 1:10; Galatians 5:14). Most notably, Jesus prays for our "complete unity" (John 17:23), and the apostle Paul reminds believers that we "are all one in Christ Jesus" (Galatians 3:28).

COMMUNITY

Before anything else, there was God (Genesis 1:1–2). As the rest of the Bible reveals, God exists eternally in three persons—Father, Son, and Holy Spirit (Matthew 3:16–17; 28:19; John 14:16; 2 Corinthians 13:14). God's "threeness" (called the Trinity) serves as a model of community for his people. In other word's, the Father, Son, and Holy Spirit live in a perfect relationship and unity with one another (Ephesians 4:4–6). If we humans are made in God's image (and Genesis 1:26–28 says we are), then we were created to live in community with God and with one another.

WHY IS THIS BIBLICAL THEME SO IMPORTANT?

Through healthy, authentic community, we reflect God's nature, bring him honor, and draw others to him (John 17:23). Not only does our community benefit us today here on earth, but it also points to our future hope of community with God in heaven.

As we think about living in community, getting along with each other and helping one another, we need to avoid the trap of thinking *unity* implies *uniformity*. Instead, the Bible celebrates diversity within our unity. For example, we each have different abilities and spiritual gifts to use for the benefit of our community (Romans 12:4–6; 1 Corinthians 12:4–11; Ephesians 4:11–13). We are one body, but we each have our own purpose and function. We shouldn't strive to copy others. Instead we should find joy and contentment in serving one another just as God made us (1 Corinthians 12:12, 15–30).

8. All will be well.

A final big idea that permeates Scripture is *the promise of restoration*. Over and over again, the Bible states that God will fix our fallen, broken world. When all is said and done, sin will be eradicated. Trouble and suffering will cease. Death will be no more. Life will finally be as God intended, forever and ever.

- In the Old Testament, God made promises (called agreements or covenants) with Abraham and Moses and David. In each case, God's desire and intent was to bless his chosen people so that they might bless the nations. In a fallen world, Israel was meant to serve as "exhibit A" to a watching world of how glorious life can be when it is lived under God's rule. The Promised Land served as a faint but tangible picture of heaven. It was "a good land" reported to be "flowing with milk and honey" (Leviticus 20:24; Deuteronomy 1:25). Most importantly, it was a gift from God. Unfortunately, the people of Israel in the Old Testament struggled to trust and obey God. As a result, they brought much unnecessary sorrow on themselves. They were removed from the land for a time. But not even that could alter God's good intent for his people.

- The prophets constantly pointed to the future. Writing to their fellow citizens who were suffering under oppressive regimes (typically because of their own disobedience), men like Isaiah saw a day when the Lord would bring ultimate judgment on evil and reign in glory (Isaiah 24:21–22; 34; 46–47; 60–66). Isaiah wrote that on that day, God "will swallow up death forever" and "wipe away the tears from all faces" (Isaiah 25:8). On that day, people will declare: "Surely this is our God; we trusted in him, and he saved us. This is the LORD, we trusted in him; let us rejoice and be glad in his salvation" (Isaiah 25:9).

- In the New Testament, God promises a future peace and eternal life for *all* people—not just the Israelites of the Old Testament. Jesus speaks repeatedly of eternal life (Mark 10:30; John 4:14; 5:24; 6:47; 10:28; 17:2–3). He calls himself "the resurrection and the life" and pledges life after the end of this life to *all* who believe in him (John 11:25–26). Just before his own death, he tells his followers that he is going to his "Father's house" to prepare a place for them, and he promises, "I will come back and take you to be with me" (John 14:1–4).

- When Jesus Christ walks out of his grave on that first Easter morning, he acts as a kind of preview of coming attractions ("firstfruits," 1 Corinthians 15:20). His resurrection shouts the truth that all those who are in Christ will live forever. What's more, we will live in what the apostle John called "a new heaven and a new earth" (Revelation 21:1).

WHY IS THIS BIBLICAL THEME SO IMPORTANT?

God's holiness means he will deal fully and finally with sin and its corrupting effects. God's grace and mercy (demonstrated in Jesus) mean that sinners can be forgiven. God's goodness means our future is one of joy and peace, not fear. God's power and sovereignty mean that he *will* restore all things. Jesus' resurrection is our sure hope. The risen Jesus gives eternal life to all who trust him. All the great themes of the Bible point forward to this one: a sure and certain future. He *is* "making everything new!" (Revelation 21:5).

At the beginning of the Bible, we see the ruin caused by sin. At the end of the Bible, we see the restoration of all things brought about by God, in Christ. Note the beautiful contrast and fullness of God's salvation.

Genesis 1–3	Revelation 20–22
"In the beginning God created the heavens and the earth" (1:1).	There is "a new heaven and a new earth" (21:1).
"God made two great lights" (1:16).	"The city does not need the sun or the moon to shine on it, for the glory of God gives it light, and the Lamb [Jesus Christ] is its lamp" (21:23).
"When you eat from [the tree of the knowledge of good and evil] you will certainly die" (2:17).	"There will be no more death" (21:4).
Satan appears and deceives (3:1).	The devil disappears forever (20:10).
Sin enters the original paradise—that is, Eden (3:6–7).	"Nothing impure will ever enter it" (21:27).
Humanity's face-to-face relationship with God is broken (3:8–10).	"God's dwelling place is now among the people, and he will dwell with them" (21:3).
Satan temporarily triumphs (3:13).	Christ, the Lamb, reigns victorious forever (22:3).
"I will make your pains in childbearing very severe" (3:16).	"There will be no more . . . mourning or crying or pain, for the old order of things has passed away" (21:4).
The earth is cursed (3:17).	"No longer will there be any curse" (22:3).
Humankind's dominion over the earth is compromised due to Adam and Eve's sin (3:19).	God's people—those who trust in him—"will reign for ever and ever" (22:5).
"The LORD God banished him from the Garden . . . [and] drove the man out" (3:23–24).	"On no day will [the heavenly city's] gates ever be shut" (21:25).
The tree of life is guarded by angels called cherubim (3:24).	The tree of life is made accessible to God's people (22:2, 14).
Humans are driven from God's presence (3:23–24).	"They will see his face" (22:4).

Rose Publishing, Inc.   May be reproduced for classroom use only, not for sale.

223

Exhibit Hall 9

Take a few moments to thoughtfully reflect on these eight key biblical themes:

1. **God *is*.**
2. **God is awesome!**
3. **People are broken.**
4. **God rescues us in Christ.**
5. **We live by faith.**
6. **This world is not all there is.**
7. **Life is a team sport.**
8. **All will be well.**

Pray that those big ideas will also undergird, permeate, and animate your life as you follow Jesus.

Afterword

Where do we go from here?

Knowing the Bible may help us impress people, win theological debates, and dominate trivia games, but that's probably not why God gave us his Word. For most Bible readers, knowledge is not the ultimate goal.

It is our hope that as you get to know the Bible, you also get to know God. We hope that as you become more familiar with the Bible's time lines, stories, and themes, you will become more connected to the Bible's Creator—your Creator.

We encourage you to take your growing Bible knowledge and continue to explore God's Word. As you read different sections of the Bible, ask yourself three questions:

- What does this passage teach me about God?
- What does this passage teach me about what God thinks of me?
- What does this passage teach me about loving others?

Learning from the Bible is a lifelong process. The more you read and reflect on God's Word, the more you can engage with it and apply it to your life. May the words of James encourage you as you continue to grow in your knowledge of God's Word:

> **"Do not merely listen to the word, and so deceive yourselves. Do what it says. Anyone who listens to the word but does not do what it says is like someone who looks at his face in a mirror and, after looking at himself, goes away and immediately forgets what he looks like. But whoever looks intently into the perfect law that gives freedom, and continues in it—not forgetting what they have heard, but doing it—they will be blessed in what they do." —James 1:22–25**

Acknowledgments

I'm amazed at the publishing team at Rose. Thank you again for your partnership and trust as we create books together that encourage people to read, engage, and apply the Bible. Thanks specifically to Jessica Curiel, Sergio Urquiza, Axel Shields, Raechel Wong, Katelyn Curran, Lynnette Pennings, and Gretchen Goldsmith.

Thanks to my agent, Dan Balow, for your hand in bringing this book to life.

Thank you Peter DeHaan and Len Woods. Your writing and editorial skills saved the day. Thanks for serving Christ our King and dedicating your skills for his kingdom.

A special thank-you goes to Robin Merrill, Mary Larsen, and Steve Leston. Thank you for your edits, feedback, and contributions.

Thank you to the Hudson Bible team. Your work and commitment inspire me.

The largest thanks of all goes to Amber. Thank you for your endless love and support.

For Further Reading

100 Prophecies Fulfilled by Jesus (Rose Publishing, 2005) – A pamphlet that lists 100 Old Testament prophecies and shows how they were fulfilled by the life and ministry of Jesus.

The 40-Day Bible Adventure: A Fascinating Journey to Understanding God's Word by Christopher D. Hudson (Value Books, 2015) - A sweeping look at the big story and big ideas of the Bible.

Christ in the Old Testament (Rose Publishing, 2009) – A pamphlet that shows how the lives of 13 Old Testament characters point powerfully to Christ.

How Jesus Changed the World: An Illustrated Guide to the Undeniable Influence of Christ by Christopher D. Hudson (Barbour Books, 2015) - A thoughtful yet readable review of Christ's effect on culture, social systems, law, education, health care, charity, even the arts.

How to Read the Bible for All Its Worth 3rd Ed. by Gordon D. Fee and Douglas Stuart (Zondervan, 2003) – Practical guidance on how to read and interpret the different genres and sections of the Bible.

How We Got the Bible by Timothy Paul Jones (Rose Publishing, 2015) – An engaging and easy read that explains how the books of the Bible were chosen and how Bible manuscripts were preserved, copied, and translated.

Rose Book of Bible Charts, Maps and Time Lines 2nd Ed. (Rose Publishing, 2014) - Clear and concise reference book which you'll find yourself going to again and again. (Also see *Rose Book of Bible Charts: Volumes 2 & 3.*)

Rose Guide to End Times Prophecy by Timothy Paul Jones (Rose Publishing, 2011) - A detailed explanation of end-times prophecy and the book of Revelation from several Christian viewpoints.

Rose Then & Now® Bible Map Atlas with Biblical Background and Culture by Paul H. Wright (Rose Publishing; published in partnership with Carta Jerusalem, 2012) – An in-depth resource for more intensive studies of Bible geography and history.

The Unfolding Mystery: Discovering Christ in the Old Testament 2nd Ed. by Edmund Clowney (P&R Publishing, 2013) - For more advanced study of typology.

Index

A

Aaron 87, 95, 106, 107, 116, 216, 218

Abel 79, 81, 95, 209

Abigail 95, 112

Abijah, King 76

Abilene 40

Abraham (Abram) 35, 36, 38, 39, 46, 52, 54, 56, 57, 67, 69, 70, 78, 82, 83, 90, 96, 97, 98, 105, 106, 109, 176, 177, 205, 214, 221

Abronah 37

Achaia 48

Acts 15, 30, 31, 49, 55, 61, 62, 63, 65, 67, 68, 69, 91, 97, 132, 136, 141, 174, 205, 212

Adam 35, 66, 70, 78, 81, 92, 94, 95, 105, 175, 194, 205, 209, 210, 211, 218, 223

Adriatic Sea 48

Adultery 80, 85, 96, 108, 113, 126, 209

Aegean Sea 48, 49, 50

Aesop's Fables 73

Ahab, King 76, 80, 97

Ahaziah, King 76

Ahaz, King 76, 96

Ain 37

Akkad 34

Akkadian Empire 36

Aleppo 48

Alexander the Great 74

Alexandria 34, 48

Alpha and the Omega 186

Amalek 37

Amaziah, King 76

Amen 148

Amman 34, 37

Ammon 37

Amon, King 76

Amos 14, 63, 68, 73, 125, 127

Ancona 48

Ancyra 48

Andrew 95, 98, 153, 200

Angels 32, 86, 94, 100, 115, 140, 144, 150, 152, 167, 183, 197, 216, 217, 223

Anna 95

Anointed One 133, 181

Antichrist 141, 148

Antioch 48

Antiochus IV Epiphanes 74

Antipatris 40

Apocalyptic Literature 16, 26, 31, 61, 148

Application of the Bible 23, 24

Arabia 48, 139

Arabian Desert 34

Arabian Sea 34

Arad 37

Areopagus 51

Ark of the Covenant 96, 109

Armenia 34

Artaxerxes, King 73, 88, 116

Asa, King 76

Ascension of Christ 44, 55, 74, 168

Ashdod 37, 40

Ashkelon 37, 40

Ashurbanipal 36

Asia Minor 43, 48, 49, 54, 72, 84, 139, 145, 146, 147, 148

Assyria 34, 73, 114, 125, 128, 129, 211

Assyrian Empire 36, 41, 65, 66, 73, 76, 96

Athaliah, Queen 76

Athens 48, 50, 51

Attributes of God 92, 208, 212

Awesomeness of God 204, 207, 208, 209, 224

B

Baal 54, 80

Baasha, King 76

Babylon 34, 35, 52, 66, 70, 71, 73, 79, 81, 115, 116, 122, 123, 124, 125, 145

Babylonia 34

Babylonian Captivity 65, 81, 82, 100, 124

Babylonian Empire 35, 36, 44, 46, 66, 73, 76, 95, 124, 129, 181

Baptism 44, 52, 57, 74, 85, 133, 151, 153, 206

Barak 96

Barnabas 75, 95, 97, 136, 144

Bartholomew 95, 98, 153

Bathsheba 80, 91, 95, 97, 98, 113

Beatitudes 133

Beelzebul 94

Beersheba 37, 40, 56

Benjamin (son of Jacob) 99

Benjamin (tribe) 44

Berea 48, 50

Bethany 40, 193

Bethel 37, 216

Bethlehem 37, 40, 44, 45, 67, 74, 79, 86, 89, 111, 128, 150

Bethsaida 40

Bible Commentaries 23

Bithynia and Pontus 48

Black Sea 48, 49

Boaz 90, 95, 111, 180

Book of Life 195, 196

Branch 182

Bridegroom 121, 183, 191

Bright Morning Star 186

Bronze Serpent 180

Buddha 73

Byblos 34

Byzantium 48

C

Caesar Augustus 74

Caesarea 37, 40

Caesarea (Asia Minor) 48

Caesarea–Philippi 40, 169

Caiaphas 74

Cain 79, 81, 95, 209

Caleb 95

Cana 40

Canaan 34, 36, 37, 39, 41, 44, 66, 69, 71, 78, 82, 85, 86, 87, 90, 105, 107, 108, 109, 110, 179

Canaanites 96, 107

Cannae 48

Canon of Scripture 18, 21

Capernaum 40

Cappadocia 48, 49

Caspian Sea 34

Chaldea 35

Cheops 36

Chorazin 40

Chronicles, First (1 Chronicles) 14, 16, 63, 68, 69, 115

Chronicles, Second (2 Chronicles) 14, 16, 54, 63, 68, 69, 72, 115

Church 13, 31, 46, 51, 65, 68, 88, 89, 99, 100, 137, 138, 139, 140, 141, 145, 148, 219

Cilicia 48, 89

Cleopatra VII 74

Colossae 48, 49, 140, 143

Colosseum 75

Colossians 15, 31, 63, 68, 75, 140

Communion (Lord's Supper) 165

Community 204, 218, 219, 220

Compassion 128, 134, 184, 210, 211

Confucius 73

Corinth 48, 50, 137, 138, 141

Corinthians, First (1 Corinthians) 15, 26, 63, 68, 75, 138

Corinthians, Second (2 Corinthians) 15, 63, 68, 75, 92, 138

Covenants 27, 61, 69, 144, 221

Creator 55, 92, 186, 195, 205

Crete 48, 100, 136, 143

Crucifixion 44, 46, 74, 134, 145, 163, 166, 167, 182, 183, 184

Cuneiform 70

Cush 34

Cyprus 34, 48, 95

Cyrenaica 48

Cyrene 48

Cyrus the Great 36, 73, 95, 116, 122

D

Damascus 34, 37, 40, 48, 74, 89, 212

Dan 40

Daniel 14, 16, 26, 27, 31, 35, 63, 68, 69, 73, 79, 98, 124, 162, 183, 215

Darius, King 36, 116

David 13, 14, 16, 18, 27, 36, 46, 53, 56, 57, 65, 67, 69, 72, 79, 90, 91, 95, 97, 98, 112, 113, 114, 115, 119, 133, 181, 182, 189, 209, 211, 214, 218, 221

Day of the Lord 126, 221

Dead Sea 19, 20, 37, 40, 41, 43, 44, 46, 52, 53, 74, 75

Dead Sea Scrolls 19, 20

Deborah 72, 96, 110

Decapolis 40

Delilah 110

Delphi 48

Demons 32, 94, 98, 154

Desert of Edom 56

Desert of En Gedi 56

Desert of Paran 37, 56

Desert of Shur 37, 56

Desert of Sin 37, 56

Desert of Sinai 37, 56

Desert of Zin 37, 56

Desert of Ziph 56

Deuteronomy 14, 28, 41, 63, 68, 69, 71, 108

Devil 94, 134, 148, 152, 175, 181, 223

Dion 40

Diversity 220

Di-zahab 37

Dome of the Rock 47, 54

Domitian, Emperor 75

Dophkah 37

E

Earth 30, 50, 52, 92, 93, 105, 133, 136, 148, 159, 162, 168, 182, 183, 184, 189, 190, 192, 195, 196, 197, 198, 205, 212, 220, 222, 223

Easter 193, 222

Ecbatana 34

Ecclesiastes 14, 29, 63, 68, 91, 121

Edom 37, 56, 127

Edomites 96, 125, 127

Egypt 34, 37, 38, 39, 43, 48, 52, 55, 66, 67, 70, 71, 72, 73, 74, 78, 85, 86, 87, 105, 106, 107, 133, 177, 209, 218

Egyptian Empire 36

Elah, King 76

Elam 34

Eli 72, 90, 96, 181

Elijah 41, 54, 56, 72, 80, 96, 97, 114, 169, 193

Elim 37

Elisha 73, 96, 98, 114, 193, 216

Elizabeth 74, 85, 96, 100, 134

Emmaus 40

End Times 26, 32, 65, 148, 161, 162, 186

En-Gedi 37, 40

Enoch 96

Ephesians 15, 31, 63, 68, 75, 139, 219

Ephesus 48, 49, 138, 139, 142, 146, 147, 148

Ephraim 40

Epibus 48

Epistles 16, 17, 26, 31, 61, 63, 69, 75, 132, 137, 141, 174, 219

Esau 82, 83, 96, 99

Esther 15, 19, 27, 61, 63, 66, 68, 73, 80, 98, 117

Eternal Life 93, 135, 146, 147, 159, 171, 180, 193, 196, 201, 221, 222

Etham 37

Euphrates River 34, 35, 52

Eve 35, 66, 70, 79, 81, 92, 94, 95, 105, 175, 205, 209, 210, 211, 218, 223

Exile 46, 66, 68, 69, 73, 81, 88, 95, 114, 115, 116, 122, 123

Exodus (book) 14, 63, 65, 68, 71, 106, 211

Exodus (event) 39, 66, 71, 87, 106, 214, 218

Ezekiel 14, 16, 63, 68, 69, 73, 81, 124, 189, 217

Ezion-geber 34, 37

Ezra 14, 17, 63, 66, 68, 73, 81, 116

F

Faith (belief) 67, 78, 90, 93, 107, 109, 118, 132, 137, 139, 141, 142, 144, 145, 147, 152, 153, 157, 158, 159, 162, 192, 201, 202, 204, 213, 214, 215, 221, 224

Faithfulness 90, 108, 109, 116, 123, 139, 156

Famine 67, 85

Fatherhood of God 92, 133, 151, 159, 160, 161, 170, 171, 195, 206, 219, 221

Fertile Crescent 52

Festival of Tabernacles 116

First Jewish Revolt 75

Forgiveness 13, 85, 93, 98, 107, 115, 143, 146, 157, 159, 160, 191, 201, 211, 213, 222

Friends 84, 87, 91, 98, 99, 118, 156, 219

Friendship 112, 205

Fruit of the Spirit 139

G

Gadara 40

Galatia 48, 49, 139

Galatians 15, 63, 68, 75, 139

Galilee 40, 41, 151

Garden of Eden 35, 66, 78, 79, 81, 94, 105, 205, 209, 211

Garden of Gethsemane 163, 165

Gaza 37, 40

Gehenna 199

Genealogy of Jesus 89, 97, 99

Genesis 14, 26, 27, 28, 60, 61, 63, 65, 68, 70, 92, 95, 96, 99, 105, 205, 209, 219, 223

Genres 16, 26

Gentiles 51, 65, 75, 97, 134

Gerasa 40

Gezer 37

Gideon 72, 96, 110

Gilgamesh 36

Glory of God 13, 54, 55, 204, 207, 208, 223

Goliath 27, 79, 112

Gomer 126

Goshen 37

Gospel (good news) 49, 51, 65, 67, 68, 69, 75, 89, 130, 138, 143, 144, 152, 157, 168, 171

Gospels (four) 16, 17, 25, 30, 62, 65, 69, 93, 132, 134, 150, 151, 154, 174, 183, 205, 212, 215, 218, 219

Grace 13, 67, 83, 88, 92, 113, 122, 126, 130, 137, 139, 147, 151, 180, 184, 199, 206, 211, 212, 213, 222

Great Sea 53

Greece 48, 50, 51, 73, 138, 140

Guardian-Redeemer 111, 180

Gulf of Aden 34

H

Habakkuk 14, 63, 68, 73, 125, 129

Hades 195

Hagar 56, 78, 90, 96, 97

Haggai 14, 63, 68, 69, 73, 116, 125, 130, 131

Hamath 34, 48

Hammurabi 35, 36, 70

Hannah 90, 96

Hanukkah 74

Hasmonean Dynasty 74

Hazeroth 37

Hazor 37

Heart 61, 80, 94, 108, 112, 113, 114, 120, 124, 126, 127, 129, 132, 140, 150, 159, 171, 174, 181, 184, 209, 212, 213, 214, 217

Heaven 74, 80, 96, 115, 148, 156, 159, 161, 162, 168, 183, 190, 192, 197, 205, 216, 217, 220, 223

Hebrews 15, 31, 63, 68, 75, 144, 176, 215

Hebron 37, 40, 79

Hell 161, 187, 197, 198, 199

Heraclea 48

Herod Antipas 74, 85, 96, 166

Herod the Great 39, 74, 96, 133, 134

Hezekiah, King 76, 96, 114

Hieroglyphics 39, 70

High Priest 73, 74, 90, 95, 96, 98, 130, 131, 166, 176, 178

Hiram, King of Tyre 72

History Books of the Bible 16, 27, 30, 61, 63, 104, 105, 132, 133

Hittites 34, 36, 71, 72

Holiness 27, 84, 107, 108, 122, 145, 205, 207, 222

Holy Land 41

Holy Spirit 12, 21, 22, 46, 74, 86, 92, 93, 131, 133, 134, 136, 150, 151, 152, 161, 168, 181, 205, 206, 219

Horeb 178

Hosea 14, 41, 63, 68, 73, 96, 125, 126

Hoshea, King 76

Humility 25, 115, 128, 140, 157, 161, 165, 179, 182, 202, 213

Hurrians 34

I

Iconium 34, 43, 48

Idolatry 67, 80, 81, 108

Idumea 40

Illumination 21

Illyricum (Dalmatia) 48

Image of God 81, 210, 219

Immanuel 150, 182

Inspiration of Scripture 10, 11, 21

Iraq 35, 43, 52, 70

Isaac 46, 54, 70, 78, 82, 83, 90, 99, 105, 177

Isaiah 14, 16, 19, 26, 29, 31, 41, 42, 61, 63, 68, 73, 82, 95, 122, 125, 167, 182, 184, 189, 207, 221

Ishmael 56, 78, 96, 97

Islam 38, 46

Island of Patmos 48, 75, 84, 148, 207

Israel (northern kingdom) 41, 56, 67, 72, 76, 114, 115, 125, 127

Israel (united kingdom) 36, 72

Italy 48

J

Jacob 38, 67, 70, 82, 83, 85, 96, 97, 99, 105, 216

James (book) 15, 63, 68, 144, 215

James (half-brother of Jesus) 15, 101, 136, 144

James (son of Alphaeus) 98, 101, 153

James (son of Zebedee) 75, 84, 98, 101, 153, 219

James the Younger 101

Jamnia 40

Jehoahaz, King 76

Jehoahaz (Shallum), King 76

Jehoash, King 76

Jehoiachin (Jeconiah), King 76

Jehoiakim (Eliakim), King 76

Jehoram (Joram), King 76

Jehoshaphat, King 76

Jehu, King 76

Jeremiah 14, 63, 68, 73, 83, 123, 182, 189

Jericho 34, 37, 40, 44, 99, 100, 109, 214

Jeroboam II, King 76

Jeroboam I, King 76

Jerusalem 30, 34, 36, 37, 40, 43, 44, 45, 46, 47, 48, 51, 54, 55, 66, 72, 73, 74, 79, 81, 82, 86, 88, 91, 95, 100, 113, 114, 116, 123, 127, 130, 131, 136, 151, 162, 163, 164, 165, 168, 199

Jesus 25, 28, 29, 30, 39, 41, 42, 44, 45, 46, 52, 53, 57, 61, 65, 67, 68, 69, 74, 84, 86, 93, 99, 100, 133, 134, 135, 140, 148, 150–171, 174–186, 189, 193, 196, 205–222

Jethro 218

Jezebel, Queen 80, 97

Joash, King 76

Job 15, 29, 61, 63, 68, 69, 70, 84, 118

Joel 14, 31, 63, 68, 73, 125, 126

John (apostle) 14, 15, 16, 31, 75, 84, 86, 98, 101, 136, 146, 147, 148, 150, 153, 197, 217, 219, 222

John, First (1 John) 15, 63, 68, 75, 146, 147

John (Gospel) 25, 30, 63, 68, 132, 135, 154, 170

John, Second (2 John) 15, 25, 63, 68, 75, 146

John the Baptist 56, 74, 85, 96, 100, 133, 134, 135, 151, 169, 177, 182

John, Third (3 John) 15, 63, 68, 75, 147

Jonah 14, 27, 53, 63, 68, 73, 97, 125, 128, 129, 184, 211

Jonathan 91, 97, 112

Joppa 34, 37, 40

Joram (Jehoram), King 76

Jordan 43

Jordan River 37, 40, 41, 44, 52, 53, 54, 69, 74, 108, 109, 151

Joseph (father of Jesus) 39, 44, 74, 86, 97, 133, 134, 151

Joseph of Arimathea 167

Joseph (son of Jacob) 38, 70, 105

Josephus 75

Joshua 15, 44, 46, 52, 63, 65, 66, 68, 71, 72, 73, 86, 95, 109, 110, 130, 131, 214

Joshua (high priest) 73, 130, 131

Josiah, King 76, 97, 114, 123

Jotham, King 76

Joy 116, 121, 139, 140, 202, 220, 222

Judah 37, 41, 79, 81, 83, 115, 123, 124, 126, 128, 129, 130, 131

Judah (son of Jacob) 99

Judah (southern kingdom) 56, 66, 67, 69, 72, 73, 76, 82, 114, 115, 122, 123, 125, 181

Judah (tribe) 44

Judaism 46, 154

Judas Iscariot 97, 98, 147, 153, 164, 165, 167

Jude 15, 31, 61, 63, 68, 75, 97, 147

Judea 30, 40, 56, 57, 74, 96, 136

Judges (book) 15, 63, 65, 68, 71, 72, 110, 211

Judges of Israel 67, 72, 110

Judgment 39, 66, 67, 82, 92, 97, 106, 122, 125, 126, 127, 130, 148, 162, 184, 193, 195, 196, 199, 211, 221

Judgment Day 195

K

Kadesh-barnea 37

Kingdom of God (Kingdom of Heaven) 133, 152, 154, 156, 157, 158, 181, 183, 189, 190, 191, 192, 204, 216, 217

King of Kings 186, 190

Kings, First (1 Kings) 15, 16, 63, 68, 69, 114

Kingship of Jesus 150, 164, 176, 181, 182, 189, 192

Kings of Israel 72, 76

Kings of Judah 76

Kings, Second (2 Kings) 15, 16, 63, 65, 68, 69, 114

King Tut 71

Kinsman-redeemer 111

L

Lake Nassar 34

Lake of Gennesaret 52

Lake Urmia 34

Lake Van 34

Lamentations 14, 63, 68, 83, 123

Laodicea 48, 49, 148

Law 13, 26, 27, 28, 42, 54, 61, 68, 69, 126, 158, 159

Lazarus 97, 98, 135, 193

Leah 83, 97

Lebanon 53, 55, 121

Leprosy 98, 100

Levi (priest) 87

Leviticus 14, 39, 63, 68, 69, 71, 107

Lion of the Tribe of Judah 186

Lord of Lords 186, 190

Lord's Prayer 133, 159

Lord's Supper 165

Lot 97

Love 107, 108, 111, 121, 123, 125, 128, 131, 134, 135, 137, 138, 139, 142, 144, 146, 147, 151, 159, 201, 205, 208, 211, 212, 213

Lucifer 94

Luke 14, 15, 16, 30, 97, 135, 136, 141, 150, 151, 163

Luke (Gospel) 14, 15, 25, 30, 51, 65, 97, 132, 134, 150, 152

Lycaonia 48

Lydia 48

Lystra 48

M

Maccabean Revolt 74

Macedonia 48, 50, 51

Magi (Wise Men) 36, 150

Major Prophets 104, 122, 126

Makheloth 37

Malachi 14, 29, 61, 63, 68, 69, 73, 125, 131

Manasseh, King 76

Manuscripts of Scripture 17, 19, 21

Marah 37

Mari 34

Mark (Gospel) 15, 25, 30, 51, 63, 65, 68, 132, 134, 147, 152

Mark (John Mark) 15, 75, 97, 134, 140, 145

Marriage 86, 121, 160, 183

Mars Hill 51

Martha (sister of Mary) 97, 98, 135

Mary Magdalene 98

Mary (mother of Jesus) 39, 44, 74, 84, 86, 97, 133, 134, 135, 150, 182

Mary (sister of Martha) 97, 98

Masada 40

Matthew (Gospel) 15, 25, 26, 30, 31, 61, 63, 65, 68, 132, 133, 147, 150, 152, 191

Matthew (Levi) 14, 15, 86, 98, 150, 153

Mayan Dynasties 72

Medes 73

Media 34

Mediterranean Sea 34, 37, 40, 41, 48, 50, 53, 128

Megiddo 37, 40

Melchizedek 98, 176

Memphis 48

Menahem, King 76

Mesopotamia 34, 35, 36, 43, 70, 78, 81, 88, 90, 105

Messiah 30, 32, 41, 42, 61, 67, 82, 99, 100, 125, 131, 132, 133, 135, 150, 164, 167, 169, 170, 176, 181, 182, 217

Methuseleh 98

Micah 14, 63, 68, 73, 125, 128

Michal 91, 112

Midian 37

Migdol 37

Minor Prophets 104, 125, 126

Miracles 41, 67, 79, 80, 85, 86, 87, 96, 133, 134, 154, 166, 182, 209, 210

Miriam 56, 87, 98

Moab 37, 56, 69, 87, 89, 108, 111

Money 142, 154, 156, 157, 160, 164, 208

Mordecai 80, 98, 117

Moses 13, 14, 18, 27, 39, 52, 54, 56, 66, 69, 71, 80, 86, 87, 95, 98, 104, 106, 107, 108, 144, 170, 174, 178, 179, 180, 205, 214, 216, 218, 221

Mt. Ararat 34, 35, 49, 54

Mt. Carmel 37, 40, 41, 54, 80

Mt. Ebal 37, 40, 54

Mt. Gerizim 37, 40, 54

Mt. Gilboa 37, 40, 54

Mt. Hermon 37, 40, 42, 55

Mt. Moriah 46

Mt. Nebo 37, 40, 43, 54, 87

Mt. of Olives 45, 55, 163, 164

Mt. Sinai 37, 54, 66, 69, 106

Mt. Vesuvius 48, 75

Mt. Zion 55

Muhammad 46

Mursilli II 36

N

Naaman 98

Nadab, King 76

Nahum 14, 63, 68, 73, 125, 129

Naomi 90, 98, 111, 180

Narrative Literature 16, 27, 28, 30

Nathan 72, 98, 112, 113, 218

Nathanael 42, 95, 98, 153

Naveh 40

Nazareth 40, 41, 42, 43, 44, 86, 151, 181, 205

Neapolis 48

Nebuchadnezzar, King 35, 36, 98, 124

Negev 37, 44, 45, 56

Nehemiah 14, 46, 63, 66, 68, 73, 82, 88, 116, 212

Neo-Babylonian Empire 36, 98

Nero, Emperor 51, 75

New Jerusalem 197

New Testament 12, 13, 17, 19, 30, 61, 63, 132, 205, 210, 212, 215, 218, 221

Nicomedia 48

Nile River 34, 37, 38, 52, 87

Nimrud 34

Nineveh 34, 43, 73, 97, 125, 128, 211

Nippur 34

Noah 35, 49, 54, 66, 70, 88, 105, 209, 211, 214

No-amon (Thebes) 34

Noph (Memphis) 34, 37

Numbers 14, 63, 65, 68, 71, 107

Nuweiba 37

O

Obadiah 14, 63, 68, 73, 125, 127
Old Testament 12, 13, 17, 19, 27, 61, 63, 104, 174, 189, 205, 214, 221
Olympic games 73
Omri, King 76
On 34, 37
Onesimus 143

P

Palestine 41
Palm Sunday 164
Pamphylia 48
Paphos 34
Papyrus 21, 38
Parables 155, 156
Paran 37, 56
Pardon 199, 200, 201
Passover 71, 165, 177
Patara 48
Paul (Saul) 13, 14, 15, 16, 17, 31, 49, 50, 51, 53, 65, 67, 74, 75, 88, 95, 97, 98, 99, 100, 134, 136, 137, 138, 139, 140, 141, 142, 143, 144, 145, 175, 186, 193, 210, 212, 217, 219
Peace 110, 133, 139, 221, 222
Pekahiah, King 76
Pekah, King 76
Pelusium 48
Pentateuch 104
Pentecost 36, 46, 74
Perea 40
Pergamum 48, 49, 148
Pericles 73
Persecution 138, 161, 162, 191
Persepolis 34
Persia 34, 73, 80, 88, 116, 117

Persian Empire 73
Persian Gulf 34, 52
Peter 11, 14, 15, 75, 89, 95, 101, 134, 136, 145, 153, 165, 166, 167, 219
Peter, First (1 Peter) 15, 63, 68, 75, 145
Peter, Second (2 Peter) 12, 15, 63, 68, 75, 145
Petra 48
Pharaoh Merneptah 72
Pharaohs 85, 87, 106, 177
Pharaoh Shishak (Shoshenq) I 72
Pharisees 89, 154, 157, 191
Philadelphia 48, 49, 148
Philemon 15, 31, 63, 68, 75, 98, 143
Philip 42, 98, 136, 153
Philippi 48, 50, 138, 140
Philippians 15, 63, 68, 75, 140
Philistia 37
Philistines 91, 96
Pithom 37
Plato 19, 74
Poetry 16, 26, 28, 61, 63, 104, 118
Pontius Pilate 74, 96, 99, 134, 135, 166, 167
Prayer 22, 24, 25, 26, 29, 55, 79, 115, 119, 133, 134, 141, 157, 158, 159, 165, 201, 206
Preservation of Scripture 21
Priesthood 144, 176
Priests 16, 18, 21, 61, 130, 131, 164, 166, 176, 185, 218
Priscilla and Aquila 99, 144
Prodigal Son 157, 212
Promised Land 41, 52, 54, 65, 68, 69, 86, 87, 95, 107, 109, 221
Prophecy 12, 16, 26, 29, 42, 61, 63, 65, 82, 104, 122, 123, 132, 133, 148, 150, 167, 183
Prophets 26, 29, 41, 68, 79, 80, 82, 96, 122, 124, 125, 128, 129, 130, 133, 162, 179, 183, 185, 216, 221

Proverbs 14, 25, 26, 29, 63, 68, 91, 120, 144

Psalms 14, 15, 25, 26, 28, 63, 68, 73, 79, 119, 211

Ptolemais 37, 40

Pyramids of Egypt 38, 70

Q

Qumran 19, 40, 53, 75

R

Rachel 83, 97, 99

Rahab 71, 97, 99, 109

Ramesses 37

Ramses I 71

Ramses II 36, 72

Reading the Bible 20, 22, 25, 27–32, 65

Rebekah 82, 83, 99

Redemption 13, 89, 111, 180

Red Sea 27, 34, 37, 39, 52, 57, 87, 106, 214

Rehoboam I, King 76

Repentance 85, 124, 125, 126, 128, 129, 152, 153, 158, 184, 199, 211

Rephidim 37

Resurrection 44, 46, 74, 94, 98, 99, 138, 163, 167, 170, 171, 184, 192, 193, 194, 205, 221, 222

Revelation (book) 11, 15, 26, 31, 46, 49, 60, 61, 63, 65, 67, 68, 69, 75, 132, 148, 182, 183, 186, 196, 205, 217, 223

Rhegium 48

Rhodes 48

Righteousness 10, 88, 119, 127, 133, 156, 177, 191, 196, 213

Roman Empire 50, 88, 166, 189

Romans 15, 31, 51, 61, 63, 75, 137

Rome 41, 43, 48, 50, 51, 73, 74, 75, 89, 136, 137, 139, 140, 142, 143, 145

Rosetta Stone 39

Ruth 15, 63, 68, 71, 72, 89, 95, 97, 98, 111, 180

S

Sabbath 108, 163, 167, 210

Sacrifice 13, 67, 107, 126, 144, 177, 201

Salt Sea 53

Salvation 28, 31, 86, 125, 126, 137, 139, 148, 157, 180, 201, 204, 211, 213, 221, 223

Samaria 30, 37, 40, 41, 44, 54, 136

Samaritans 41, 54, 135, 156

Samosata 48

Samson 72, 99, 110, 113

Samuel 65, 72, 90, 96, 112

Samuel, First (1 Samuel) 15, 63, 65, 68, 69, 72, 112

Samuel, Second (2 Samuel) 15, 63, 65, 68, 69, 113

Sarah (Sarai) 36, 56, 78, 82, 90, 96, 97, 105

Sardis 48, 49, 148

Sargon 36

Satan 81, 84, 94, 118, 152, 175, 223

Saul, King 36, 54, 56, 57, 65, 67, 72, 80, 90, 91, 97, 112, 113, 136, 214

Savior 13, 86, 92, 124, 134, 150, 154, 168, 184, 186, 195, 196, 217

Scapegoat 178

Sea of Galilee 37, 40, 41, 43, 52, 53, 167

Sea of Tiberias 52

Second Coming of Christ 141, 145, 148, 157, 161, 162, 174, 190, 202

Seleucia 40

Septuagint 74

Sermon on the Mount 133

Servanthood 30, 51, 57, 97, 134, 182

Seven Churches of Revelation 49, 148

Shallum, King 76

Shang Dynasties 71

Sheba 34

Shechem 40

Shepherd 45, 79, 112, 119, 125, 156, 170, 185, 189

Shiloh 37, 72

Shinar 35

Sicily 48

Sidon 34, 37, 40

Silas 99, 136, 141

Simeon 99

Simon the Zealot 98, 99

Sin 80, 107, 110, 113, 115, 123, 126, 137, 140, 146, 157, 160, 175, 177, 178, 180, 192, 196, 204, 209, 210, 213, 223

Sinai 37, 55, 56, 87, 106, 107

Sinful Nature 209, 210

Sin Offering 178

Sinope 48

Slavery (slaves) 38, 39, 51, 66, 74, 85, 87, 98, 106, 143, 177

Smyrna 48, 49, 148

Solomon, King 14, 36, 44, 46, 54, 65, 67, 72, 79, 91, 95, 113, 114, 115, 120, 121, 214

Song of Songs 14, 26, 28, 61, 63, 68, 73, 91, 121

Son of God 30, 53, 92, 132, 135, 170, 175, 205, 206, 219

Son of Man 124, 134, 163, 170, 180, 183, 184, 212

Sovereignty of God 84, 92, 122, 208, 222

Sparta 48

Spartacus 74

Stephen 74, 99, 136

Stonehenge 70

Succoth 37

Suffering 65, 84, 118, 123, 138, 145, 161, 175, 182, 198, 211, 212, 221

Sukkot 116

Sumer 34

Sumerian Empire 36

Sumerians 35

Suppululiuma I 36

Susa 34, 80, 117

Sychar 40

Synagogue 42

Syracuse 48

Syria 35, 40, 48, 52, 53, 55

T

Tabernacle 69, 71, 87, 90

Tamar 97, 99

Tarsus 34, 48, 89

Temple in Jerusalem 23, 46, 49, 54, 61, 66, 72, 73, 74, 75, 91, 95, 99, 114, 116, 123, 125, 130, 131, 151, 154, 163, 164, 176

Temple Mount 47

Temptation of Jesus 56, 57, 152

Ten Commandments 56, 66, 71, 87, 108

Tetrarchy of Philip 40

Textual Criticism 18

Thaddaeus 98, 99, 153

Thessalonians, First (1 Thessalonians) 15, 31, 63, 68, 75, 141

Thessalonians, Second (2 Thessalonians) 15, 31, 63, 68, 75, 141

Thessalonica 48, 50, 141

Thomas 98, 99, 153, 167, 184

Thrace 48

Thyatira 48, 49, 148

Tibni, King 76

Tigris River 34, 35, 52

Timnah 37

Timothy 100, 138, 139, 140, 141, 142

Timothy, First (1 Timothy) 15, 63, 68, 75, 142

Timothy, Second (2 Timothy) 15, 63, 68, 75, 142

Titus 15, 63, 68, 75, 100, 138, 139, 143

Torah 104

Tower of Babel 35, 67, 70

Transfiguration of Christ 55, 80

Translation of Scripture 21

Tree of Life 223

Tree of the Knowledge of Good and Evil
79, 81, 223

Trinity 92, 93, 206, 219

Tripolis 48

Tripolitania 48

Triumphal Entry 164

Trojan War 72

Truth 11, 18, 21, 22, 23, 24, 60, 83, 123,
127, 137, 138, 146, 147, 152, 155, 156,
170, 171, 174, 183, 188, 199, 208, 222

Turkey 35, 43, 49, 52, 53, 54, 72, 139

Twelve Disciples 13, 67, 74, 95, 98, 99, 101,
133, 134, 135, 153, 164

Twelve Tribes of Israel 13, 44, 52, 83, 86,
106, 209

Typology 174

Tyre 34, 37, 40, 48

Tyrrhenian Sea 48

U

Ugarit 34

Ur 34, 35, 36, 52, 70, 78

Uriah 80, 95, 113

Uzziah 76, 100, 114, 115

V

Veil 176

Vine 170

Visions 11, 16, 79, 81, 124, 148

W

Wedding 157, 183, 191

Wilderness of Judea 40, 56, 85

Wilderness Wanderings 66, 71, 107

Wisdom Literature 26, 29, 61, 63, 104, 118

Worship 31, 39, 61, 69, 84, 94, 108, 119,
130, 138, 140, 150, 183, 197, 206, 208,
211

X

Xerxes, King 73, 80, 117

Y

Yeast 157, 158, 191

Z

Zacchaeus 100

Zarephath 40

Zechariah (father of John the Baptist) 96

Zechariah, King 76

Zechariah (prophet) 14, 31, 45, 63, 68, 69,
73, 74, 85, 100, 116, 125, 131, 134,
164, 176, 182, 184

Zedekiah (Mattaniah), King 76

Zephaniah 14, 63, 68, 73, 125, 130

Zerubbabel 46, 66, 73, 100, 116, 125, 130,
131

Zhou (Chou) Dynasty 72

Ziggurats 70

Zimri, King 76

Ziph 37, 56

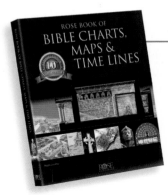

Rose Book of Bible Charts, Maps & Time Lines
– 10th Anniversary Edition

Dozens of popular Rose Publishing Bible charts, maps, and time lines in one spiral-bound book. Reproduce up to 300 copies of any chart free of charge.

- Christianity, Cults & Religions
- Denominations Comparison
- Christian History Time Line
- How We Got the Bible
- Tabernacle
- Jesus' Genealogy
- Bible Time Line
- Bible Bookcase
- Bible Overview
- Ark of the Covenant
- Islam and Christianity
- Bible maps
- Trinity
- Temple and High Priest

Includes MORE pages, 6 EXTRA topics, updated information, and a bonus 24" fold-out on Jesus' Family Tree. Hardcover with a spine covering a spiral binding. 230 pages.

ISBN: 9781596360228. Product Code: 314X

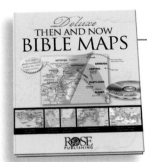

Deluxe Then and Now® Bible Maps
Book with CD-ROM!

See where Bible places are today with *Deluxe Then and Now® Bible Maps* with clear plastic overlays of modern cities and countries. This deluxe edition comes with a CD-ROM that gives you a JPG of each map to use in your own Bible material as well as PDFs of each map and overlay to create your own handouts or overhead transparencies. PowerPoint® fans can create their own presentations with these digitized maps. *Deluxe Then and Now® Bible Maps* uses larger, easier-to-read type than most Bible atlases. Hard-cover spine with spiral interior. 40 pages – double the content of the original.

ISBN: 9781596361638. Product Code: 629X

Bible Overview

The Bible has over a thousand chapters, and this book will help you get a quick introduction of each of its sixty-six books. This full-color guide gives you a fantastic 2-to-6 page overview of each book of the Bible, and includes...

• Purpose of the book and how it fits in with the rest of the Bible • The author • The date the book was written, and to whom • Key themes and key verses • Summary of the key teachings and an outline of the stories in the book • Maps, time lines and photos
• Explanation of how Jesus can be seen in each book • Applications for God's people today. Reproducible, full color, paperback. 266 pages.

ISBN: 9781596365698. Product Code: 168X

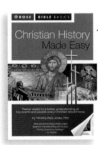

Christian History Made Easy

Summarizes the most important events in the history of the church, from the time of Jesus to modern day. *Christian History Made Easy* explains early church history, the Church Councils, the Great Schism, the Crusades, Francis of Assisi, John Wycliffe, Martin Luther, the Protestant Reformation, and more. *Christian History Made Easy* presents key church history events and great Christian leaders everyone should know, along with full-color church history time lines, photos, pictures, and maps. Paperback. 224 pages.

ISBN: 9781596363281. Product Code: 705X